I Can't Fix It ... but I Know Who Can

SANDRA STILL

ISBN 978-1-64349-910-9 (paperback)
ISBN 978-1-64349-911-6 (digital)

Christian Faith Publishing, Inc.
832 Park Avenue
Meadville, PA 16335
www.christianfaithpublishing.com

Cover Photographer: Cherrie Hair

Printed in the United States of America

To my dear friends Kenneth and Joan Pressey, two of the most courageous, optimistic, and inspiring people I have ever met. Their unwavering faith in God has been an example to many.

Contents

Introduction

---◆◇◆---

The Lord is my light and my salvation—whom shall I fear? The Lord is the stronghold of my life—of whom shall I be afraid?

—Psalm 27:1

Life—living—is a problem, and we just can't fix it. We can't control it. We can't perfectly understand it. The past is often a puzzle. The present is a challenge. And we can't with certainty plan for the future, as the future simply has too many what-ifs, unknowns, and variables. Further, when we do look at our life options, why is it we often focus on the bad, difficult, horrible possible outcomes? In my experience, I rarely awaken at 3:00 a.m. filled with awe and excitement over all the possible good, positive, upbeat outcomes that may lie ahead. (Ah, I assume the "evil one" is actively at work in this area.)

The Problem, with a capital *P*, is life, plain and simple. Illness, death, loneliness, divorce, children who break our hearts, friends and family from whom we are alienated. So many issues! Career challenges—or a lack of career in the face of job loss. Politics, wars, natural disasters, the list of earthly woes is endless. We can't fix them, but I know who can.

This book looks at forty-nine different situations I have experienced either firsthand or through the lives of friends and relatives. They are meditations, a word which in Hebrew doesn't necessarily mean quiet contemplation. Rather, the root word for *meditate, hagah,* often meant "to moan, utter aloud, muse, and just plain mutter"; "to roar"; "to growl"; "to speak out"; or in short, oftentimes "pure lamentation and calling out to God." Forty-nine reflections on woes and finding God's love within them. As you read these musings, take time to ponder the closing questions for each entry. All of them may not personally apply, but all will offer ideas to consider. Also pray the suggested short prayer or, better yet, form your own prayer thoughts and express your own groanings and thanksgivings to the Lord.

The fiftieth entry is different. It puts the emphasis on Jubilee. In the Old Testament, guidelines for the newly established Jewish nation directed that every fiftieth year was a time for rest, renewal, and celebration. And so the fiftieth meditation does just that—celebrates the Lord's goodness and provision for his people. We of the New Covenant, the Church, can face life's trials and hardships knowing that one of these days Jesus's promise, "I am making everything new" (Revelation 21:5), will come to pass. In Christ's kingdom, there will be jubilee. No weeping, no sadness, no illness, no aging and decline, no death. There will be joy as we live in the presence of God himself. Pure, unfettered, limitless, abundant joy.

And so let us begin the journey of meditating on life's challenges, knowing that we can't fix it but focusing always on the One who can.

Section 1

---◆---

Be Still

*Be still and know that I am God; I will be exalted
among the nations, I will be exalted in the earth.*

—Psalm 46:10

A Quiet Mind

❖

You will keep in perfect peace those whose minds
are steadfast, because they trust in you.

—Isaiah 26:3

I am tired, Lord. And not because things aren't going well. Actually, they are going well overall, excepting a few blips here and there. It just seems I've been striving so to serve you, and now my reserves are gone. I'm sitting at the lake on this Sunday morning instead of being in church, because I just can't face being in a crowd of people. I don't want to hear about one more person's needs. It's not that I don't care! Actually, I think I care too much. The prayer list grows relentlessly, and I *care*!

But … I can't fix any of it. A sense of powerlessness engulfs me. Pray. Just pray? What good does that seem to do? Okay, then, along with prayer, I need to act. So I do—endlessly seeking to do more, more, more. And now I am really, really tired. Besides taking energy, actions also, for the most part, don't seem to achieve much. So I feel like I'm basically accomplishing nothing by praying and doing. What's left?

Then I read Isaiah 26:3. God will keep me in perfect peace *if I trust in him*. Uh, oh … there it is. I don't really *trust* God. I find it difficult to put people and problems totally in God's hands, with the trust that he will work all things together for good to those who love him. The realization comes: my anxiety, tiredness, and frustration at root come from pride.

What is that feeling of "I must stay involved with a person distressing my soul if they are to turn to God" but pride. *Me*—I am essential to success. Right? No, I don't think so. I'm praying for them

11

but also feeling I must *do something*! "Here, Lord, I'll help you lest things go wrong …"

Is my worry and fretting essential for the physical healing of those on my prayer list? Probably not. Yet to pray for them and then, in joy, go on with the day's tasks the Lord has provided for me seems, well, coldhearted. Now is that way of thinking not the opposite of God's instructions to cast my cares on him and to then walk in peace?

Eliminating this problem will take prayer and practice, for fretting, worrying, and second-guessing "in the name of the Lord" has obviously become a deeply ingrained habit. Also, prayers of repentance at my prideful attitude apparently need to be part of my daily routine for a while. And instead of wearing myself down with frenzy and fretting, perhaps using that energy to joyfully take flowers to someone homebound or to quietly visit a friend better serves.

Why, what an eye-opener! There are peacefully done acts of concern I can do, instead of worrying, rushing frantically, and fuming over a "grand solution"; so let me be about them with a sense of trusting God, not one of breakneck, exhausting agitation. Instead of weariness of spirit, Lord, grant me your peace. Let me turn from an introspective focus on myself to outward focus on prayer and then thoughtful quiet action. It sounds like a plan, because in my heart of hearts, I know "I can't fix it, but I know who can."

Reflection

- Make a list of things you "do for the Lord" each week. Now prayerfully analyze your list. Ask God if this activity is truly his will for you.
- Conversely, is your list lacking in acts of service? Be in prayer that the Lord will open doors of opportunity for you to better serve him.

Prayer thought: "Dear Lord, show me the way you wish to use me in your service at this stage and time of my life. Amen."

Hope

*In His great mercy he has given us new birth into a living hope
through the resurrection of Jesus Christ from the dead.*

—1 Peter 1:3

She sat contentedly across from me in the sun, comfortable on the
picnic table bench. The empty fast-food paper bag that had held
hamburgers and fries now was stuffed with empty wrappers and cups
destined for the trash can.

"It's so beautiful here." She sighed. "I didn't know there was
such a lovely spot so near my house." Overwhelmed, I gently patted
my mom's hands as they rested on the picnic table.

"I know, Mom. Isn't the lake peaceful?" She smiled at me, her
eyes lit with happiness. "Ah, Mom. I have been visiting you for
almost a week, and every afternoon, you and I have come here. My
childhood days were filled with many picnics enjoyed in this same
spot with you, up here on this hill. My brothers, sisters, and I walked
the lake's shores with you watching over us. It's always been your
favorite spot.

"Now, each time I bring you here, it is a new spot, a new adventure for you. Ah, Mom—dementia is slowly taking your mind, your
memories, and my heart. And yet there is such happiness here for
you because, each time we come, it is like the first time. Every day all
things are special and new through your eyes. Being with you, doing
things with you, helps me to see the ordinary through your childlike
viewpoint. That is a great gift, a great blessing even amidst the long
sorrow of seeing you slip away."

Then, and even now years later, my aching heart asks the Lord,
"*Why?*" Why do you allow the misery of dementia, of Alzheimer's

disease? It seems one of the cruelest afflictions, incredibly hard on both the sufferer and those who love them.

Hope, Lord. You don't answer my why, but you give me hope, as you do others coping with these circumstances. Lord, what is there but hope? Not hope for a recovery (though any miracles would be appreciated) but hope for patience. Hope so that we who believe in you can cling to your promise. The promise that in your kingdom, there will be no disease, no sorrow, no suffering, no slipping gradually away to an unknown.

Lord, help me, help us, to embrace your hope, embrace your promises, with all our hearts. "Weeping may stay for the night, but rejoicing comes in the morning" (Psalm 30:5). Give us hope, dear Lord. Come, Lord Jesus. Let the dawn begin.

Reflection

- Are you, or someone you know, coping with a seemingly hopeless situation? What, specifically, is it, and how is it affecting you?
- If possible, praise God for the good moments that have come from this tragic situation. What were some unexpected times of sharing and inspiration?

Prayer thought: "Father, Papa, the sorrow I feel as I reflect on this hard situation could cause me to despair. Please, Lord, show me that you are there through it all and that there is hope in you. Amen."

Know Thyself

◆—◇—◆

When he, the Spirit of truth, comes, he will
guide you into all the truth ...

—John 16:13

I sincerely wish I—we—had the ability to clearly see ourselves, to truly know ourselves. In observing my life and the lives of others, it is obvious what a difficult task this is. "Behold, I think I am cooperative and thoughtful!" Uh oh. My sister assures me I can be overbearing and controlling. Who? Me? Perhaps she is right, but I just don't see it. Exactly!

We want to give, help, be thoughtful and charitable; the recipient thinks we are being patronizing and maybe even insulting. Is that, perhaps, the truth? We don't want to think so, but then again ... it is just very hard to tell. We want to encourage others to volunteer, be a tutor, work in the hospital, man a food pantry, so we share our experiences. At which point someone comments, a bit bitingly, on all our "good works." Well, we sincerely want to promote opportunities, but how can we do that if we "do not let your left hand know what your right hand is doing" (Matthew 6:3)? Our motives are pure ... we think ...

We want to be there for others, help them, listen to them, advise, and cajole. And then we go home wondering if we were honestly sharing or were we rather being manipulative, thereby adding to their stress as we attempted to tell them what to do. I don't know! Sometimes, I just honestly don't know. Given our incredible tendency to deceive ourselves, I lament, "What is truth?"

Jesus said the Holy Spirit will guide us into the truth. Repeatedly, the Bible assures us we can know the way, and Jesus will help us.

It seems to be a slow, steady process rather than an instantaneous, overnight miracle (though that does sometimes happen). I think of Mary and Martha when frustration looms. Martha was so busy, so dedicated. She had a servant's heart and deeply wanted things to be done just right. And Mary, sitting there apparently doing nothing, was not right!

"Lord," Martha wailed, "tell that thoughtless girl to get in here and help me!" Imagine her total shock when Jesus praised Mary for making the better choice. What? Martha's world view just got flipped upside down. Priorities suddenly dramatically shifted. Martha had to learn to be still and sit at the feet of Jesus (Luke 10:38–42).

We experience life, and we do learn. Perhaps on this venture, project, or visit, my intentions were good; but I was too brusque in speech, a bit too pushy. Ouch. Time to apologize and next time, to approach a task in a more cooperative spirit. Okay, yes. I know I have a generous heart and want to share, but is it remotely possible I also need to let others share with me? Give to me? Help me? As a frustrated friend once rather firmly told me, "Would you please just give me the gift of helping you?" That was a powerful thought, a new thought that contained enormous truth. If we don't graciously receive, how can someone else have the joy of giving?

Are we volunteering, doing good works, for the correct motive? If we lay aside telling others what we are doing, will we continue to carry out our "good works"? No glory, no one knowing except the Lord and those directly involved? Would that change things for us?

Truth is, we need to be open to what God puts before us, pray, and trust the Holy Spirit to guide our thoughts, words, and actions. Truth is, even as we blunder along, God will honor our attempts in spite of mistakes we may make. Better to do something as opposed to doing nothing, and trust the results to God. "Being confident in this, that he who began a good work in you will carry it on to completion until the day of Christ Jesus" (Philippians 1:6).

Reflection

- List several areas of service you engage in. Why do you enjoy being involved in them?
- Now ponder and reflect. What, as far as you can determine, is your true motivation for doing these things? Is your motive good and pure, or do you suspect you have an alternative reason? Be honest.

Prayer thought: "Lord, help me desire to serve you according to your leading, with a pure heart and sincere motivation. Amen."

Which Way Should I Go?

*Therefore do not let anyone judge you by what you eat
or drink, or with regard to a religious festival …*
—Colossians 2:16

I t is one of those behaviors or activities that I'm not even sure is an actual sin. In fact, it well may not be, but I'm just not sure. It may be a sin for *me* to pursue while perfectly permissible for someone else. It actually has health benefits and can be a positive addition to life, but, again, some believers would adamantly say no.

A good many activities or behaviors can fit this description, can't they? I once heard a story about how, during a break at a missions conference, German church leaders sat in the local beer garden, with their craft beers and cigars, earnestly discussing the questionable dietary practices of their "too chubby" American colleagues. While elsewhere, at the same time, a group of conservative American leaders sat over coffee and pastries discussing the evils of alcohol and smoking! One Christian's vice may be another's fulfilling pursuit.

In the apostle Paul's day, the eating of meat sacrificed to idols was one of those "search your souls" issues. Some believers felt meat was meat, and as everyone knew idols were totally fake, anyway, what was the harm? Enjoy that prime rib! Other believers recoiled in horror, deeply convicted that Christians buying such meat were supporting idol worship. Flee from even the appearance of evil!

Hummm … shall we dance? Take in a movie? Use contemporary music in worship service? Visit and witness in bars or clubs to be where the unsaved are likely to be? A little brainstorming would turn up numerous examples of "we're not sure" activities. But here's the point. How do we know what is permissible for us or what we need to turn away from, barring a clear condemnation of said activity in scripture? As we consider the issue, it is equally important to focus on ourselves, given that what we feel led to reject might be perfectly fine for our fellow Christian to pursue.

In my case, after wrestling with the issue for quite a while and doing a considerable amount of rationalizing, I came up with questions that helped clarify the issue. First, was the behavior causing me uneasiness in my relationship with God? If so, why? Was the unease due to past training or teaching that may well have been illogical or overly restrictive? Well, perhaps so. But even after a period of examination in light of Scripture, the uneasiness remained. Was continuing the behavior worth it, given my doubts? Do I need to do more searching of the scriptures?

Secondly, was I handling it well, with pure and acceptable thoughts and emotions? Now there was a problem: as along with positive, acceptable thoughts, there also seemed a portal for darker, less-than-godly thoughts. The behavior was probably, in and of itself, a neutral, but my responses often were not. Did I want a possible portal opened for Satan to worm his way in?

Thirdly, and ultimately, did the positives of the behavior prove necessary to my Christian life and witness? Will letting it go cause inconvenience or harm? A small price to pay for peace of mind? Or is that being overly restrictive and in bondage?

We all must be sensitive to Spirit's leading in our lives. I can tranquilly stroll amidst the gallery of Rodin nude statues at my local art museum entranced by the sheer beauty of the works. My dear friend hurries through when we visit, as she is overwhelmed by lewd, lustful thoughts and needs to just meet me later at the café. One dear saint can count the offering plate donations with nary a thought of "all that money," while another person might be overcome with thoughts that "no one would ever know if I ..."

Activities and behaviors can be neutrals, but our responses often are not. As children of God, let us be aware of temptations that appeal to our weak areas. When we pray "lead us not into temptation," we must be sure we don't then turn from our prayers only to indulge in something questionable for us. May we all walk in love for God and our fellow believers.

Reflection

- Carefully consider areas in your life and activities that make you uneasy as you walk with God. Why do you feel uneasy? Are your reasons valid?
- Prayerfully lay the issue before the Lord. Search scripture and perhaps consult with other Christians. Be open to God's leading.

Prayer thought: "Lord, deliver us from evil and protect us from the evil one. Help us to know what is good and acceptable to you. Amen."

Press Pause

❖

Be still before the Lord and wait patiently for him ...
                                                                    —Psalm 37:7

Patiently. Now there's an aggravating word if there ever was one. In fact, it's right up there with *wait*. We—I—do not like being a creature bound by time. The older I get, the more I feel time is a limited, precious commodity. "Let's not waste it," I fret.

Knowing the limitations, we—I—often embark on a frenzied round of "do-itis." Pack more into each day; that's the ticket. Make that "to-do" list ever longer—impossibly longer, impressively longer. All the better to beat ourselves up with when we can't get it all completed. And why is the list not completed? We run out of physical, mental, and emotional energy. "Wait," Spirit says. Unfair. The determination is strong, but the flesh is weak. We must stop to rest. And time marches on ...

Wait also frustrates us in other areas of life. A friend called to the mission field has fretted her way through language school and cultural training. Should I even mention the hours she has spent waiting patiently in airports as she flies on standby in order to save money? There's something to try one's soul!

Who hasn't waited patiently for an illness to run its course or an injury to heal? Or perhaps the health problem becomes chronic, demanding that patience and quietness of spirit be developed for a lifetime. Patience to learn how to maneuver crutches, a wheelchair, or hoists and lifts. Patience as others must be relied upon for caregiving and relief. The spirit is willing but the weak flesh just cannot carry on!

Patience makes great demands on those working with the mentally ill, dementia patients, and developmentally handicapped children. Oftentimes, there's no reward of seeing improvement, and time itself seems mocking as it brings nothing but the sameness of deterioration. Wait patiently for what? Death? So it seems.

The disciple Peter struggled with this concept from his earliest beginnings in his walk with Jesus. When Jesus called to him, "Follow me ..." Peter immediately left the boat and nets to set out. During the great storm at sea, when Peter saw Jesus walking toward them on the water, the impatient Peter shouted, "Lord ... order me to come to you on the water!"

"Okay, Peter, come on out ..."

Out jumped Peter; bravely, he walked toward Jesus ... until fear raised its head and Peter began to sink. Fortunately, Jesus knew his friend well and was quickly able to come to the rescue (Matthew 14:28–31).

And then that horrible, dark night when the soldiers came for Jesus and he was led away. All seemed lost. What point was there in patiently waiting to see what God had planned? It was obviously over, and Peter's despair overwhelmed him. Twice he said, when asked, "No, no. I do not know him." The third time, someone came up to him and said, "You really are one of them too. Even your accent gives you away."

At that, Peter's patience totally evaporated, and "he began to call down curses, and he swore to them, 'I don't know the man!'" Lacking patience, unable to wait to see what God had in mind, Peter denied. Then, realizing what he had done, he went out and wept bitter tears (Matthew 26:73–75).

Let us rest in the Lord. Let us press pause now and again. The truth is, time applies only to our time on planet Earth. We are actually eternal beings, and eternity lies before us. God has tasks for us to perform and complete while we are here, and he gives us the strength and energy to do them. However, he also repeatedly tells us to rest in him, to go away at times to a solitary, quiet place. To be still. To wait patiently. Let us be at peace.

Reflection

- Assess your personality. Are you by nature tranquil and peaceful? If not, how do you tend to approach life and its endless demands?
- Look up three or four scripture verses that speak of patience and peace. Jot them down so you can refer to them in times of turmoil.

Prayer thought: "Ah, Lord. You made us and know us, that we are prone to fuss, fear, and fume. Enter my heart that I may be sensitive to that still, small voice calling me to rest in you. Amen."

Weary

Never tire of doing what is good.
—2 Thessalonians 3:13

The sheer needs in life, in society, totally overwhelm at times. It's too much, and our contributions at alleviating that need seem so little. I grow weary; we grow weary. Where should our efforts be applied? The food bank? The job training programs? Tutoring struggling youngsters? Cleaning a sick friend's house? Training a therapy dog? Serving in a ministry? *Stop!* The list is endless, and we grow weary just trying to decide where to serve.

We pray, "Lord, please lead me and show me your will, and help me to recognize the path I am to take." We know not what else to do as we rush frantically from one good cause to another, exhausting ourselves, neglecting family and home. Surely, this is not the answer. Yet that's often the path we fall into.

"Be still, and know that I am God" (Psalm 46:10). Stop. Rest. Regroup. It is not our responsibility to do it all, to rescue the world. We are a part of the body of Christ; we are a piece of the entire puzzle. Faith is surely required if we are to relax and prepare each day to do our part, trusting God to bring all things to fruition. Thinking "I'm not doing enough. There's so much need" may be true if we are living selfishly, actually doing very little. However, for those sincerely reaching out, seeking God's will and way, the "I'm not doing enough" attitude may be an indicator of pride raising its ugly head. I—the great I—must save the world.

No. That's Jesus's role, and he has taken care of it. God has tasked some of his children to be powerful preachers speaking to large audiences. And God has tasked some of his children to labor—mostly forgotten—on lonely mission fields with few converts to show for their work. Some organize vast projects of aid to those experiencing the disasters of floods, earthquake, and war. Others give a cup of cold water, a word of encouragement, a humble contribution.

Lord, help us to not grow weary in well doing and to ever seek your still, small voice as we seek to serve. Also, protect us from the attacks of Satan who, seemingly, delights in whispering his lies in our ear. "You are pitiful and your efforts pointless. What do you really do? God is disappointed in you. Do more. Work, work, work. However, it is to no avail, for my capacity for evil in this world is endless. Why not just weep and give up?"

Yes, oh Lord, protect us from the lies of Satan, and help us to see that we do make a difference, whether our "good works" be grand and visible, or humble and quiet. Peace.

Reflection

- What is your favorite way to "be still"? Where do you go to retreat and reflect?
- How might you reconcile "never tire of doing what is good" with "be still and know that I am God"?

Prayer thought: "Father, remind us that you are in charge of this world, not us. Help us to wait patiently for your still small voice and to then act according to your will. Amen."

Aging—'Tis a Challenge

Even to your old age and gray hairs I am he,
I am he who will sustain you.

—Isaiah 46:4

"Old age isn't so bad when you consider the alternative." Probably a famous quote from someone, but in my life, it's a bit of my dad's philosophy. The older he got, the more he said it. Until that sad day came when he shook his head slowly and whispered, "I'm ready for the alternative now."

I do not like aging one bit. Not for my parents, my friends, my colleagues, or myself. Golden years, indeed. Why God designed life to grow old, decline, die, and decay is beyond me. Suffering, humiliation, loneliness, and rows of old people languishing in senior citizen homes—what is the purpose, Lord?

And then it hits. This is *not* what God designed, is it? No, it is not. God intended that we were to be perfect, eternal beings fellowshipping with him. That was the plan … and then Satan worked his deceptions, and, well, here we are.

Almost everyone has a story to tell, a memory of Grandma, Great-grandma, Mom, or Dad. Questions, heartbreaking questions such as that asked by my remaining uncle at my mother's—his sister's—funeral. All his large family of siblings were now gone; only he remained, sitting in his wheelchair after the service. Looking at us, tears running down his face, he asked, "Why? Why am I still here?"

"I don't know, Uncle Curt. I don't know," I replied sadly.

The Lord was merciful and heard his lament, for within six months, he left this earth for his heavenly home, but the "why" still lingers.

This aging process doesn't just affect the elderly. Friends and family often must step in and take up the slack. Someone has to do the taxes, pay the bills, keep up the home for the one in decline. Who is going to arrange for a place in assisted living? Who can take in Uncle Bert and give him a back bedroom? Anyone have granddad's power of attorney? Guess I'm going to be caregiver. Does that mean my life is over as I know it? I worked my entire life to retire and enjoy some golden years, and now this? How totally unfair it can seem.

Of course, there are blessings amidst the heartache. Golden moments of quality time listening to the wisdom of the elders. Shared times of laughter and remembering. Visits with shut-ins where their joyful spirits and wonderful attitudes lift the soul.

The truly wise begin to realize aging is a time of increasingly letting go. In downsizing a home, one lets go of physical property no longer needed. One sheds the second car as a spouse loses the ability to drive. Unnecessary possessions are given away. Gradually, business and household accounting gets turned over to trusted others. Control wanes. Control over one's mobility, wealth, time, and activities. Pride must yield to increasing humility.

For those who know Jesus and trust in him, this letting go is surely easier, for we put our loved ones and ourselves in his hands. As our earthly life and activities shrink, our view of the eternal expands and grows. Here on this earth, we can't fix this aging business, but God surely has got this! Death does, indeed, lose its sting. Goodbye, creaky old physical body. Hello, perfect heavenly body. We can't fix this, but we know who can.

Reflection

- Consider where you or loved ones are in life. Is aging becoming a concern? What challenges seem to lie ahead?
- Amidst all of life's problems, how has God sustained and blessed you? Think of several specific incidents and take time to give thanks to the Lord for his love and care.

Prayer thought: "Lord, I come to you a human, earthly being, facing earthly death at some point. And yet, Lord, I praise you for redeeming me, that I may live eternally with you. Thank you, Lord. Amen."

Stop Fighting

*Woe to those who quarrel with their Maker ... does the
clay say to the potter, "What are you making?"*

—Isaiah 45:9

Time to stop fighting. No, that does not mean it is time to give up, but rather it is time to stop striving and to let God be God. To stop fretting. To say, "Your will be done," and mean it. For I am weary and tired of being constantly agitated. My lifelong, prideful compulsion to ever achieve is just exhausted. And, ironically, at the end of a day filled with self-imposed deadlines and lists completed, there is not contentment. Rather, there is the wearying awareness that yet another list looms for the morrow. So it goes, day after day.

Time to stop fighting. To accept where God has currently put me and what he has provided for my hand to quietly do this day. To look to God for balance, realizing that while I may feel compelled to accomplish ten tasks, he may be asking me to do only one or two things. Then, perhaps, he would enjoy me just peacefully contemplating him and his word.

Time to stop fighting, but do not give up! Clearly, God gives his children tasks to tackle. We are to assist others, show compassion, work diligently to develop, and use our talents as the Lord leads us. He is instructing me to do all these things in his timing, not mine. To realize the rests in the musical composition are as important as the crashing crescendos. I chafe at the rests; let me at the crescendos, Lord! Bring on the sound and the fury ... oops. All that commotion might, in truth, signify nothing, right?

Day-to-day routine. Patiently caring for what God has blessed me with. Tending babies. Caring for a sick person. Cleaning the house and taming the lawn. Preparing lessons, cooking meals, cleaning up afterward. Shopping, washing clothes, making a nice home. "Lord, listen. The true action is out there in the big world, not here at home, at my dull place of work, or doing endless chores. Come on! Hustle, bustle, let's get a move on …" If I had been Moses, I'd not have lasted even one year out there with the sheep, let alone forty, waiting on the Lord to put me into the game.

Why is it that quiet appreciation of the blessings he has showered upon me doesn't seem to be enough? The truth, perhaps, is that, in spite of my saying I believe I'm saved by grace and mercy, I'm actually convinced in my heart that I must earn my place in heaven. I think I must constantly do more. Or could be there is an even harder truth. My restless mind is in a quest of the next adrenaline rush brought on by deadlines, crisis, tough problems to master—even if I must create them myself. Perhaps, in reality, I dread boredom and the routine of life. Being still before the Lord—that's very hard.

Time to stop fighting. Time to experience life as the Lord slowly unfolds it, responding as he leads and tending to the work he clearly sets before me. Time to stop always questioning his judgment, his timing, his fairness. Time to stop asking why and being agitated at things I don't understand and cannot affect. Time to live in harmony and peace. May it be so.

Reflection

- What is there in your life that you need to stop doing? How do you know? What is God showing you?
- Knowing and doing are two different things, but we must try. In what way can you seek God's will in these matters? What steps might you take?

Prayer thought: "Dearest Father, you know I am but clay in your hands, and yet in my pride, I constantly try to tell you what I want to be used for and what I want to do. Help me, Father, to just rest contentedly as you mold me with your capable hands and wise wisdom into a vessel fit for your kingdom. Amen."

Section 2

---◆◇◆---

My God, My God ...

My God, my God ... why have you forsaken me?
—Matthew 27:46

Back Against the Wall

———◆◇◆———

Well done, good and faithful servant! You have been faithful
with a few things; I will put you in charge of many things.

—Matthew 25:21

Back against the wall, I slowly slid down to the floor, tears flowing. Right there. Right there in the busy hospital corridor between the chapel door and the large floor-to-ceiling windows where the sun streamed in.

"Lord," I whispered, "Lord, I can't do this. Why is all this happening? I can't handle it all. I simply can't." My mind went numb; my thinking stopped. The hall was sunny, but all seemed dark. No one stopped to see if I was all right; probably sobbing people slumped against walls in a hospital weren't all that uncommon.

The dark night of the soul. Not so much the illnesses looming over me, but the bewilderment that God was allowing all this to happen to me. It wasn't that I didn't trust and have faith; I was just too crushed. I felt I couldn't rise again.

Of course, I eventually did get to my feet and make my way home. One does, somehow. Weak, so sick, as it was my second day after yet another round of chemotherapy for my recently diagnosed invasive breast cancer. Face red and flushed, head spinning, tired beyond tired. I'd left my husband behind in the hospital. He had just been told he needed heart bypass surgery immediately, as in *tomorrow*. Care for myself? Care for him in his six-week recovery? Continue to work at my job, a necessity to stave off financial crisis? Where was God?

Many years later, I still don't clearly understand his purpose in allowing that dreadful time of life, and I have talked with others who have gone through the fire with God's help but who also still haven't figured out the "why." Oh, yes, many survivors of tragedy do have the privilege of saying, "Oh, now I totally understand God's purposes ..." I'm not one of them.

However, what I do know is that God did sustain me. He did send people who made my recovery, without financial disaster, possible. He did give me strength and comfort in the long lonely nights. And in the past years since that incident, the Lord has filled my life with amazing ways to serve him, as well as blessing me endlessly. God is good—always.

When I—you—walk through the Valley of the Shadow, there is one thing we can know absolutely. It will be worth it all. We will see Jesus. He will welcome us with those blessed words, "Well done, good and faithful servant." The hurt and pain will be remembered no more, and we will dwell in the house of the Lord forever.

Reflection

- In time of great trouble, in what ways do you reach out to God, seeking his help?
- Clarify your thinking, as much as possible, as to why you think God allows his people to suffer through horrendously difficult times. Take time to research Bible passages to support your thoughts.

Prayer thought: "Lord, oftentimes we, like Job of old, simply suffer and do not understand. Be with us, Father, when our grief is so overwhelming we cannot even find the words to pray. Hear Spirit as he prays for us. Be with us and comfort us. Amen."

Good in Affliction?

It was good for me to be afflicted so that I might learn your decrees.
—Psalm 119:71

Afflictions have a way of getting our attention, don't they? Busy, busy, busy. The day, the week, the month, and the year are all laid out in our notebooks and planner calendars. We are good to go ... until we're not.

I hate it when an affliction of some sort rises up. Plans and routines get disrupted, and the stress rises. Anger, too, often announces its presence. "Oh, great, just great. Now I have to make arrangements, haul someone to the emergency room, and wait, wait, wait. And child care? Jobs? Why me!"

How about resentment and fear? "Why, God, do I have cancer? I take care of myself, and I serve you faithfully and *this* is *not* fair. Do you understand how disruptive this will be? Do you get it, Lord, how afraid I am?"

Long-standing afflictions also take their insidious toll. Conditions present from birth. Constant abuse in the life of a child. Horrible diseases such as ALS or Parkinson's with progressive decline. What possible good can come from such afflictions? When you begin working with or talking with afflicted people, the stories of blessings from trials you often hear inspire. The verse from Psalms states a benefit—that we may learn God's statutes.

Currently, I am working with a friend who delights in sharing the miracles of God's healing in her life. After a lifetime of abuse, rejection, and coldness from her mother, she has worked this past year or so at learning and understanding God's statutes on forgiveness. As she has day-by-day practiced forgiving, to her surprise, she has experienced a great desire to use her affliction to go and serve others in some way. Her goal? To bring good from bad. Multiply her a thousand times over. Cancer patients, both those in remission and those who are terminally ill, frequently reach out to others in ways only someone who has "walked in those shoes" can. Those who were, or are, dealing with poverty learn God's statues of concern for the poor by volunteering with food banks, clothing ministries, and other outreach organizations.

People brought low learn God's statutes about self-reliance and pride. Often having reached a point of total despair, the folly of "I can overcome everything by myself" becomes achingly apparent. Then, in the darkness, they cry out to God—and thereby change their lives for all eternity.

Granted, not all people gain from affliction. Many curse God in bitterness and tears. Others, even when the situation improves, forever cling to resentment and self-pity, determined to be victims for life. The key to weathering affliction successfully is a willingness to seek the Lord's face, knowing that with God all things work together for good to them that love him. And note, this verse does not say all things *are* good, rather that God can bring good out of all things.

Affliction can be absolutely horrible. Let's not sugarcoat that. At the same time, let us use each trial in life as an opportunity to seek God and grow.

Reflection

- Consider a past affliction in your life. Difficult childhood? Unhappy marriage? Disease? Other loss?
- Ponder what good has come out of that ordeal. How did you gain or grow from it?

Prayer thought: "Father, protect us from afflictions in life. However, Lord, if they come let me trust in you, that good will come. Amen."

It Will Be Okay If I Only Believe ...

---◆◇◆---

Do not be afraid of what you are about to suffer ... be faithful, even to the point of death, and I will give you life as your victor's crown.
—Revelation 2:10

"If I pray hard enough, with enough faith, I will be delivered from suffering." So goes our thinking, many a time, as Christ followers. We read verses about blessings, happiness, joy, deliverance; and because *this life, this world* is the only one we are familiar with, we expect the good here and now. However, our expectations are clearly unfounded in biblical truth. Yes, we may experience much good and many blessings in our earthly life, for which we are to be grateful. But carefully consider the example on which today's Bible verse is based.

In this passage, the church at Smyrna (an ancient city in today's Turkey) has been praised for their faithfulness while living amidst a sea of evil. Persecution, prison, death loomed all around, yet they remained faithful. Surely, they would be delivered from all harm! Evidently—*not*. As unthinkable as it may be, instead they are told, "You are about to suffer even more," to the point of death. Wait, what?

We begin to realize as we grow in grace, God isn't focused on our lives *in this world*. From his perspective, our eternal lives with him in his kingdom are what really matter. Consequently, on earth we often suffer, and we pray for deliverance. Of course, we also want to define exactly what that deliverance will consist of! Death comes, and we ask, "Why didn't God answer our prayers?" Ah, but we forget, in our grief, that for God's children death leads not to the endless grave but rather to the crown of life. The earthly death of our loved one in Christ is but the doorway to their glorious life with the Lord.

Of course, we know not all those whom we love are in Christ, and for them, our fervent prayer is that they may know the Lord, and thereby also be promised a crown of life. We throw ourselves on God's great mercy and wisdom. And therein, also, lies great suffering for us that demands our faithfulness and trust.

We grieve. We suffer. We ask why. God understands we are but dust and limited in our vision. However, as we grow in him to where we can accept suffering as an inexplicable part of life, we can, indeed, remain faithful and walk confidently through death's dark door into our real, heavenly home.

Reflection

- What event(s) of suffering have you experienced in life? Jot several down.
- In what way did these experiences affect your growth in the Lord?

Prayer thought: "Father, as I struggle with suffering and trouble in this life, hold me in your hands and give me hope. Amen."

Why, Then, Does Love Hurt So?

◆◇◆

Dear friends, let us love one another, for love comes from God.
Everyone who loves has been born of God and knows God.

—1 John 4:7

Why does love hurt so much? Not just "bad" hurts, but also "good" hurts. I hold my little dogs and feel such a love for them, my heart aches, and tears fill my eyes. The emotion is almost more than I can bear.

Most parents hold their little babies and are overwhelmed with the aching desire to protect and nurture. Teachers look into the eyes of students they have grown to love, and the longing to protect and guide brings tears of joy and, often, frustration. Grown children hold the hand of a failing parent with a grief so deep, a love so strong it can hardly be borne.

Why does love hurt so much? Is it not supposed to be a joyful, fluffy, fun emotion bringing song and laughter? Obviously, something beyond our popular understanding is at work here. For the flip side of "good" love is invariably grief. We can't escape it or change it unless we simply harden our hearts. If we would never acquire a pet, get close to a child, stay involved with our friends, care about a parent—then we would be safe. Ironically, however, such a "safe" life would bring its own overwhelming loss and grief.

Why does love hurt so much? Though I have no definitive answer, I think it is because in this life, in this world, people and animals die. And in our souls, we know this is *wrong*! God created his world and all things in it to live. Death is a lie. Death is evil. Death brings grief to our souls. In the very act of loving, we open ourselves to the pain.

Thanks be to God, he understands this. The Holy Spirit strengthens us to endure our suffering and our grief upon the death of the beloved. God knows how we feel. His great love and grief were demonstrated at the suffering and death of Jesus. When he created us, God knew that he and we would endure such pain due to our love. He created us, anyway. And so, likewise, we open ourselves to love, knowing it will hurt. We cherish our dear pets, our children, our students, our friends, and our parents, knowing they may be gone from us at any time. And we love, for God gives us the courage to love.

"For God so loved the world that he gave his one and only Son, that whoever believes in him shall not perish but have eternal life" (John 3:16).

Reflection

- Remember those people, animals, and things you have greatly loved—and lost.
- How did you find solace as you struggled with grief? If you are still struggling, what steps might you take to work through your sorrow?

Prayer thought: "Our compassionate Father, be mindful of our human frailty in the face of loss and grief. Help us to ever trust in you for comfort. Amen."

Hopeless

For you know that the testing of your faith produces perseverance.
—James 1:3

H er beloved son, twenty-something, suffers with a mental illness. There seems to be no help and no hope. It's affecting her
family. This woman doesn't want to go home to a husband angry and
stressed from dealing with his belligerent out-of-control child. She
realizes she has deliberately become overly involved in church activities in an effort to appear justified in neglecting her family. When
she shared this information with her church small group, it obviously
hurt her. Honesty often isn't easy.

She feels frustrated, unsure, hopeless—caught in a situation
impossible for her to control. It just seems to go on and on and
on. Does she continue to help her son? Or should she stop, practice
tough love, and watch her son possibly self-destruct? All of us in the
group around that table felt such compassion and sadness. We can't
fix it; she can't fix it. However, we all know who can.

And yet, as we prayed—some with tears and a quaver in their
voices—I sat there and wondered if God really will do anything to
help. I have such faith in God, but sometimes I have trouble with
trusting him. Mental illness is totally daunting and devastating. How
do you reason with someone unable to logically reason? Healing
rarely seems to happen, despite the impassioned prayers of friends
and family. It appears to take a miracle ... Lord, will you work a
miracle? I—we—know you can. But seemingly you rarely do. You
desire for life to unfold for us humans slowly day by day. And that's
hard, very hard. It requires great patience; it requires trust and faith.

Lord, I believe. Help my unbelief. Have mercy, Lord, on those who struggle with mental illnesses. Help their families to patiently live day by day. Help them to discern between helping their ill, struggling loved ones and enabling the person's destructive behavior. Help their hurts to be healed with love, even as they insist the ill person seek treatment and take responsibility.

Peace, Lord. Bless them with your peace, for those dealing with the mentally ill often experience hopeless turmoil and despair. Help parents, caregivers, friends to learn that the day-by-day process, the journey, is what is important because the goal of everything being "all better" and healed may never happen in this lifetime.

Help them, help all of us, focus on *this* day. Not yesterday, not tomorrow. *This* day. Give us strength to meet today's challenges and trials. And especially, Lord, give us the ability to experience joy at each day's good things, good moments, and simple routines. For today, this day, is your gift to us.

Reflection

- Do you, or someone you know, struggle with mental illness or addictions? What, specifically, seems to be the main problem? How does it affect your life?
- List coping skills you use, or can begin to use, that will help you calmly face each challenge day by day.

Prayer thought: "Father, dealing with this burden is wearying me. Please give me the strength and wisdom to deal with these challenges and teach me to totally trust you. Amen"

I Don't Understand

---◆◇◆---

*Trust in the Lord with all your heart and lean
not on your own understanding.*

—Proverbs 3:5

"I don't understand!" The soul cry of many a bewildered person in the face of life's challenges. Often, nothing seems to make any sense to us. "Why are things working out this way?"

Are these the cries of an unbeliever berating God? Oftentimes, no. Rather, they are the cries of believers, of those who have sacrificed much in a fervent desire to serve the Lord. And then ... it all falls apart. The plans go horribly awry, and we struggle. After all, we were seeking to follow and serve, and this is our reward?

My "hit the wall" time came after my first year teaching high school. I'd worked incredibly hard to go back to college later in my life, giving up a successful small business. Without a doubt, God had laid it on my heart to be a teacher; nothing could not be overcome to gain that magical degree. Success, my first teaching position, a school I liked ... and a layoff notice early in May. A layoff notice!

"God, I have sacrificed much to follow your will and now—this?" Last hired, first fired, and the district faced financial difficulties.

On the way home that afternoon, I stopped by my church, literally sank down on the altar steps, and sobbed. All this effort to now be unemployed? God became very real in those moments as the sovereign Lord—a being whose mind I could not grasp. Where was the Santa-God who would acknowledge my great labors with deserved reward?

And so, I and others prostrate our panting souls at God's feet, not understanding. The faithful pastor who, after years of scholarly service, develops dementia. The unwavering father who endures summer's blistering heat to work daily putting on roofs and, after retiring, develops a melanoma on his "hammer-holding" wrist that spreads mercilessly and kills him. The nurse who tirelessly and voluntarily cares for Ebola patients but then develops the disease. The examples are endless. Obviously, many times the adage "No good work goes unpunished" seems quite, quite true. Consequently, we need to notice that "Lean not on your own understanding" is proceeded by "Trust in the Lord with all your heart."

Ah, there lies our answer, our hope, our solace. Trust in the Lord—just trust. We don't need to question, to dissolve in tears, to rage in anger, to vow God is a cruel God. May we just trust. With all our hearts. Trust.

Reflection

- Is there an area of resentment toward God that you have not fully acknowledged or dealt with? What is it? What exactly are your feelings regarding it?
- Pray earnestly. Tell God frankly how you feel, why you feel that way; ask him to help you to let go and trust.

Prayer thought: "Lord, help me to express to you my sincere anger and bewilderment. You know I love you, but these feelings persist. Hold me close, forgive me, and help me to truly trust you. Amen."

Enough Is Enough

Weeping may stay for a night, but rejoicing comes in the morning.
—Psalm 30:5

He has been in cancer treatment for a while. It has been rough, especially given an allergic reaction he had to one of the chemotherapy drugs. Changes were made, and things got tolerable, but treatments also had to increase in frequency, allowing him little recovery time between rounds.

And then his mother died. I can't help it, Lord, but my first reaction was "Enough is enough!" Furthermore, he is not the only Christian I know who seems pushed beyond endurance. I've been there, for one, along with many others.

When we decided to take up our cross and follow Jesus, did that include painting a bull's-eye target on our backs for Satan to aim at? Sometimes, it sure seems like it. What should we—can we—make of these recurring phenomena? Well, I sure don't know ... end of meditation. But wait!

Job asked God this question, the "why," and got no answer. God answers the "why" by insisting we be humble, praise him, and trust. The apostle Paul asked for his thorn in the flesh to be removed. It wasn't. The answer to the why? God answered, "My grace is sufficient for you ..." (2 Corinthians 12:9).

We cannot understand the ways and the mind of God. "'For my thoughts are not your thoughts. Neither are your ways my ways,' declares the Lord" (Isaiah 55:8). To begin with, we absolutely lack the big picture of purpose that God is constructing. This life, to us, is very important. Eighty years or so is a lifetime to human beings. (It is, bear in mind, no time at all to a sequoia tree!) To our thinking,

45

we must get well *now* so we can move on. Things need to fall into place *today*, lest we get behind. Suffering is all fine and noble for, say, three or four days, but after that, others begin to regard us as wimpy, whiney fellows.

God's will unfolds at his pace in our lives. He weeps with us as illness, decay, and death thwart our lives and threaten to steal our joy. However, he also knows it is a temporary condition, and in his good time, he will make all things new. During a season of sorrow, the Lord sustains us, holds us, walks with us. Let us sorrow, but always with hope and joy in our hearts, knowing that "to live is Christ and to die is gain" (Philippians 1:21). We can't lose!

Reflection

- Think of a weakness or problem that you, or someone you know, struggle with in life. What specific difficulties does this problem present?
- Reflecting patiently, can you see a way in which this weakness or problem has been beneficial and used of the Lord?

Prayer thought: "Father, how I want to escape from weaknesses and problems. Like Paul, I request they be removed from me. But, Father, you know best. Give me the ability to trust you always. Amen."

A Man of Sorrows

◆◇◆

He was despised and rejected by mankind, a man
of suffering and familiar with pain.

—Isaiah 53:3

"Would you like to know exactly how you will die, what the end will be like?" How many of us would say yes to this question? Think about it ... Would you *really* want, right now, the revealing of that mystery?

On the plus side, you could plan accordingly and—possibly— live each day to the fullest. If you're one of those people, I admire you. On the other hand, I suspect many people are like me. While I'd like to think I'd live each day to the fullest, in my heart, I suspect I would live each day with an ever-increasing sense of doom. As in, "In fifteen years, I'll be ... Oh, now in fourteen years, three hundred and sixty-four days, I'll be ..." And so the dreaded countdown would continue. No, I do *not* want to know the day nor hour nor method of my leaving this earthly life!

Jesus knew. He *knew*. Give that serious thought. At some point, as he grew from baby to manhood, it became clear to him. He was going to put himself out there in a demanding, controversial ministry. He was going to be betrayed to his enemies by a supposedly close friend. Humiliation awaited at the mocking, cruel hands of so-called religious leaders. People spitting on him, placing thorns on his sensitive scalp, flogging him with cutting barbaric whips.

And then the ultimate degradation—being nailed to a cross and hanging for all to see. The pain, the shame, the total sense of abandonment by God and mankind loomed ahead. And every day, as he taught, healed, laughed, lived, he knew the time was one day closer.

It bothered him; it weighed on him. In the garden of Gethsemane, he prayed for another way. Then, accepting the inevitable if mankind was to be saved from eternal condemnation, he prayed for courage. The Valley of the Shadow had to be walked through. For Jesus, as it will for us, a time arrived when there was no other way.

He was a man of many sorrows, well acquainted with many griefs. He knew the horrible future even as he began his earthly journey. "Ah," some may say, "but he also knew God would raise him up again."

Yes, he did. And so do we. We know we shall rise again as Christ followers into eternal life with our Lord. Does that knowledge make facing death any easier? Most assuredly so. And yet the sorrow, fear, and grief of death remains. We cry for understanding, deliverance, and strength, as Jesus on the cross cried out to God. And the words echo back to us, "Yea, though you walk through the Valley of the Shadow of Death, I—the Almighty God—am with you."

Reflection

- Seriously consider. Would you want to know the time and method of your earthly death? Why or why not?
- How might that knowledge affect your day-to-day life?

Prayer thought: "Dear Lord, thank you for living boldly and facing the ordeal of the crucifixion so that I might face earthly death with courage and hope. Amen."

Section 3

◆◇◆

Trust in the Lord

*Trust in the Lord with all your heart and lean
not on your own understanding ...*

—Proverbs 3:5

Life's Universal Challenges

◆◇◆

I have told you these things, so that in me you may have peace. In this world you have trouble. But take heart! I have overcome the world.

—John 16:33

Frankly, it gets tiring, doesn't it? The endless, ongoing, pervasive parade of sorrows in this life. Seems like the only defense at times is to withdraw into one's private world and shut out all the bad news. I've more than once stopped listening to the news and "reading all about it." But escape is impossible, for try as we may, sorrow and trouble persist in invading our circle of friends, our family, our church, and ourselves.

Seems at times that my prayer list for others gets so long, I'd just best throw it away and pray "for everyone in this world." How many soup kitchens and food banks can we donate to or volunteer for? How many hospitals, nursing homes, retirement communities can we visit? How many condolence messages, letters to prisoners, and encouragement cards can we write?

Currently, on my neighborhood street alone live a widower, a family who recently lost a mother, a family whose child committed suicide, an older woman struggling after a hip replacement, a man losing his legs due to diabetic complications, and next door— an empty house whose aging resident now lives in an extended care home after a fall.

What a mess! And yet life goes on. The widower is active in his church. The motherless one praised God at her mother's funeral. The parents of the deceased child walk their dog and wave cheerfully. The hip-replacement lady uses her walker and sits on her front porch in nice weather, happy to chat. The wife of the diabetic invalid, beauti-

51

fully dressed, heads to church each and every Sunday morning. The man from the empty house next door? His sons care for his house and give encouraging reports on his adjustment to assisted living.

How can these things be? How is it our neighborhood is one of encouragement and joy, instead of sorrow and despair? Why is there love and hope in this bleak, brutal world? Observe—listen—question, and we find that God is in the hearts and minds of his people. Through them, in big ways or small, Jesus makes manifest his peace in the midst of troubles. No, we *cannot* avoid the problems of life in a sinful, fallen world. But we can live blessed in his assurance to "take heart, for he has overcome the world." Peace.

Reflection

- What are some issues in life that puzzle you or bring you to despair? Be specific.
- What goodness in life brings you hope and renewal? Be specific. In what ways can you express your joy in spite of trouble?

Prayer thought: "Dear Father, bring peace to my heart in times of distress, and remind me that I can always rest in you. Amen."

I Can Fly

❖

Do you give the horse its strength or clothe its neck with a flowing mane?
—Job 39:19

I eat a simple breakfast, then drive to the barn where I stable my horse. Today will be spent with friends and horses. Like knights of old, my *Cowboys for Christ* friends and I set out to do battle against the pain, hurt, and despair in life. Today, we load up our horses to go give "pony rides" to children facing their own private battles. Our task—to show God's love through our horses.

God seems to take special pride in his creation—the horse. I understand why. Powerful, skittish, intelligent—yet they will submit themselves to the requests of humans. My horse, PixieJoy, leaves her green pasture to come greet me. I look into her large dark eyes and sometimes feel I can see a disguised angel looking back. Who are these creatures so beloved of God? Who am I to be blessed with the trust and companionship of such an animal?

The diesel truck engines come to life; our caravan pulls out. God's countryside scrolls by. Today, our battle against illness and suffering is at a special picnic for autistic children. How many questions arise! Why, Lord? Why are these children faced with such challenge? Why must these parents struggle so? I have no answers, but I do have my patient mare.

The sun rises higher in the sky; the temperature climbs. Children are lifted onto our horses, side walkers take their places, and off we go. I carefully lead my horse, who seems to understand how precious the children are who perch on her back. It seems like I have walked a hundred miles, round and round. The children laugh, giggle, or stand mute, remote and unresponsive. Sweat runs down my shirt.

Sometimes working to better the world is just plain hot, repetitive, exhausting; there is no glamour.

The unresponsive young boy is lifted on PixieJoy's back, and we set off slowly around the field. By now a path has been worn in the grass from many hooves. PixieJoy knows the routine. Plod, trudge, sweat. Suddenly, without warning, the unresponsive child rises up from his slump and sits straight. His arms slowly rise from his sides and flutter into airplane wings position. His clear voice lifts toward the afternoon sun.

"I can fly! I can fly!" he shouts. His mother, walking alongside, gasps as tears begin to run down her face. "He never speaks," she whispers. "He never speaks."

"I can fly! I can fly!" he crows over and over as Pixie carefully walks on.

In a world of pain, suffering, and unanswerable questions, my friends and I go out to do battle. God puts those in my life whom I am meant to touch that day. And the horses—God's horses—humbly walk on. Back at the barn, I hose PixieJoy down, then turn her out to enjoy her hay. Once home, I sit quietly in the yard, watching the day draw to a close. The great horned owls who live in my neighbor's trees eerily hoot back and forth to each other. The light fades, and the bullfrogs once again pick up their booming songs. The birds have fallen silent. My spirit soars. "Oh, Lord," I pray, "I shall rise up and tell of my love for you!" In answer to all the questions—there is God.

Reflection

- Do you, or someone you know, struggle with issues such as autism? What are some of the special challenges involved?
- Think of a time when you were able to serve or help others in a special way and felt very blessed. Ponder God's goodness in allowing you take part in his great work.

Prayer thought: "Dear Father, thank you for the times, big and small, when you involved me in doing something to assist others. Open my heart to your leading that I might constantly work with you. Amen."

Essential Loneliness

I will not leave you as orphans; I will come to you.

—John 14:18

We all carry, at core, a sense of loneliness. And many of us also carry a longing to be home with the Lord—a void unfillable on this earth. Research increasingly shows humans function best when interconnected, living in community. Connections are vitally important. And yet, if one talks to the most connected of people, often they will express this loneliness inside.

Oh, it may not be a tragic feeling of "no one loves me," though it can be that powerful. Usually, it's just a sort of aching longing for an undefined "something." What is that something? Ah, there is the puzzlement. Checklist time. Friends, a few close ones or many—check. Family, both near and far—check. Acquaintances, to swap stories with, say hi to, get help from as needed—check. A purpose in life, others to assist, teach, work with—check. Parties, picnics, gatherings, holiday celebrations, sporting events, walks in the park, other things to do. Check.

And we are lonely. Some days, some mornings, some afternoons, some evenings—just lonely. There may be people near, far, all around ... we are lonely. We watch the sun come up; we watch the sun go down. Feeling lonely. The day is filled with business and chores, or it may consist of reading a good book in front of the fireplace. Feeling lonely. What *is* this ache? This longing?

We miss fellowship with God in our lives, I believe. Now wait. Before protesting "I know God. I read my Bible and pray daily," consider. Those activities are very important and very real times that help ease that lonely spot, but that's not quite what I am getting at.

Direct, in person singing of "holy, holy, holy" with the saints in heaven. *That* is, I believe, our deepest longing. As Paul said in 1 Corinthians, "Now we see through the veil darkly, but then face to face." That's what our souls long for … face-to-face.

When the time comes—either through our death or at Christ's return—that we at last go to be with him in his realm, that lonely feeling will be vanquished. We will be filled with his love and Spirit. Furthermore, we will truly know others, and they will truly know us. Misunderstanding, guardedness, boundaries of fear or unease will fall away.

Then the true connectedness will be evident, and we shall be lonely, sad, melancholy, longing no more. It will be unimaginable and deeply satisfying. No longer lonely. "Come, Lord Jesus!"

Reflection

- What are the times in your life when a sense of loneliness seems to hit? What do you believe causes this?
- Consider your feelings about heaven and being with the Lord. Do you long for it, pray for it?

Whom do you hope to meet there?

Prayer thought: "Lord, my soul longs to be in close fellowship with you, free from the cares and restraints of this earthly existence. May you come soon and take us home. Amen."

God with Us

———◆◇◆———

Never will I leave you; never will I forsake you.
—Hebrews 13:5

B etween bouts of quiet tears, the frail ninety-plus-year-old patient interacted with my little therapy dog, Brella. Leaning back in the hospital reclining chair, with Brella on her lap, she told me how she had outlived her siblings, had no children, and only a niece and nephew who lived some distance away. She needed surgery, but her doctors felt it was too risky, and so she was going to a hospice center the following day. When the time came for us to leave, she softly sobbed, "I wish I had a little dog. I'm so lonely." My heart just broke. When the visit ended, my assistant and I went into the hall and paused to weep, overwhelmed with sorrow.

"Lord, please be with that dear lady! Don't abandon her! Lord, why must we age, decline, and suffer such loneliness?"

It is worth pondering that even the apostle John, last of Jesus's earthly "inner circle," is said to have wondered why his life on earth continued, for he longed to go home to his Friend and Lord.

Admittedly, part of my sorrow as I walked away down the hospital hall was for myself. Will that be me, in an all-too-short span of years? Easier to turn away, to not visit the ill, the old, the lonely. We don't want to be reminded that, barring the Lord's return for his church, we face either decline or avoid it by an earlier death. And with either option, we make the journey alone, even if others sit by our side.

Or do we? In that hospital room, that dear lady felt lonely, and yet she also spoke of her church and her faith. Jesus repeatedly assures us he will never leave us alone. "I will not leave you as orphans; I will come to you" (John 14:18). How he does this is sometimes obvious as people enter our lives to give hope and comfort, even as I, my assistant, and the therapy dog were sent to visit that dear lady.

Sometimes, God's presence is obvious, evidenced by peace in the night allowing the distressed one to sleep and rest. In many cases, his care comes by allowing death to release the suffering one into his eternal life. Regardless, many events in life are too hard for us to begin to understand, but the Lord knows exactly what he is doing, and his timing is always perfect.

"I will never leave you ..."

Reflection

- Have you experienced being with an aged person as their earthly life draws nearer to its close? What emotions did they, and you, experience?
- How has God made his presence known to you in difficult situations?

Prayer thought: "Our Father, draw near to those who are in life's twilight. Comfort them and calm their fears. Send your people to them, to assure them they are not forgotten and alone. Amen."

What If ...?

———◆◇◆———

Preserve sound judgment and discretion ... when you lie down, you
will not be afraid; when you lie down, your sleep will be sweet.
—Proverbs 3:21–24

Unfortunately, my sleep is not always sweet precisely because I am afraid. How about you? It's one thing to read and agree with all the many Bible verses telling of God's care and provision. It seems to be quite another matter to consistently reject fear and worry.

Part of it is an unwillingness to embrace the idea that God's care does *not* mean we will have no hardships. Rather, the promise is that God will be with us *through* whatever life throws at us. Oh no! That's not the promise I want to hear, that God will be with me when life gets tough. I—are you listening, Lord?—want to be shielded from all hardships. And that's what provokes fear and worry at 3:00 a.m. many a night. What if ...

What if a loved one develops dementia, requires extensive care, and eventually drains a lifetime's worth of finances?

What if I become ill or disabled, and no one comes to my assistance?

What if I have to sell the house and go to assisted living some-day. Where and how would I begin?

What if ... a child becomes terminally ill, employment is lost, a flood comes, or a tornado hits?

And I dare not try to escape my fear by turning on any type of media! Now the entire world's horrors join the local herd of anxiet-ies. Deranged terrorists, earthquakes, wars, endless sinfulness. Yikes! Turn it off, quick!

And, of course, it all seems much worse late at night, in the dark, alone with one's thoughts. The mind races, the pulse rises, and

59

sleep flees. What happened to "when you lie down, you shall not be afraid."

I have found several coping methods that usually help. First and foremost, pray! "Lord, I am having a panic attack here, and I need your help to just be at peace and get back to sleep." Secondly, a touch of humor can assist. I tell my racing mind and frightened spirit, "Okay, let's go with this. I am going to meditate upon every single verse I can think of that tells me to be afraid and trust in my own understanding to reason things out." Now *that* didn't take long, did it?

Thirdly, start mentally, silently, singing a hymn or a song, that expresses God's goodness and deals with trust. Over and over, I "play" the selection in my mind. Fourthly, and most importantly, meditate on, think about, a verse or verses that assure us God *is* with us and does walk through the hard times, holding us in his hand. "Even though I walk through the darkest valley, I will fear no evil, for you are with me …" (Psalm 23:4).

Hopefully, sleep will return quickly as panic subsides. If not, then I just quietly think on the Lord and count the awake time as an opportunity for prayers. Often, in that situation, profound thoughts and answers to prayer come to mind.

"Keep sound wisdom and discretion …" Let's knock on his door about our restlessness, and wisely ask God for peace as we seek his purpose. Good night!

Reflection

- What time of night (or morning) seems to consistently be your "wake-up call?" List some of the thoughts or emotions that are often in your mind when that happens.
- Consider the list; specifically think about how likely these things are to happen. For the likely ones, prayerfully think of ways the Lord will help you cope should they come to pass.

Prayer thought: "Father, hold me in your love when I awake in the night, mind racing and emotions out of control. Let me know your peace. Amen."

Weaker by the Day

---◆◇◆---

My grace is sufficient for you, for my power is made perfect in weakness.
—2 Corinthians 12:9

Friends and family know, barring a miracle, our dear friend's outcome. Decreasing muscular strength, lost function, and eventually death. He knows it, as does his wife. Diagnosis—ALS (amyotrophic lateral sclerosis).

One would logically expect despair, anger, resentment, and grief in such a situation. At first, and still at times, it was and is there. But now, several years into the ordeal, there is primarily joy, humor, perseverance, and love. Much love. A *lot* of love for God, each other, family, and friends.

Recently, they celebrated their fifth anniversary; it was very special, considering they married after he found out about his condition. She said the ALS made no difference to her, and she was willing to cope with what was to come.

And so she gladly and cheerfully feeds him, dresses him, keeps him clean and comfortable, and fills his days with interesting activities. They prepare Bible lessons and host a small group in their home every week. Sundays, she helps him into their customized van, and they attend church. The big question—"Why us?" Both agree they are beyond asking that anymore, just accepting that they—and we— live in a fallen world full of problems and troubles. Or, as he often says, "Why not me? Am I somehow special?"

Well, yes, he is. They are. Their amazing example of acceptance and faith is a witness that can't be ignored. Their light of Christian faith shines bright. A favorite scripture verse clarifies their position:

"My grace is sufficient for you, for my power is made perfect in weakness."

Skeptics sometimes state that anyone may profess to be a Christ follower when all is going well. However, when they meet and talk with two people being faithful despite such daunting challenges in life, the same skeptics are puzzled. The testimony, the belief, of this strong couple makes a tremendous impact on a disbelieving world. Their peace, their joy—how can this be? God's grace is sufficient.

Reflections

- Think about someone you know who faces overwhelming problems yet their faith in God remains strong. What is their explanation for their faith?
- What is their impact on you? What specific qualities about them speak to your heart?

Prayer thought: "Lord, give strength, peace, and joy to those coping with seemingly impossible situations. Be mindful of their struggles and bless them. Amen."

Divorce

I have great sorrow and unceasing anguish in my heart.

—Romans 9:2

Marriages—relationships—die. So many reasons, so many causes. Major issues such as unfaithfulness, abuse, violence. Minor reasons like "I just don't want to be married anymore." Regardless, the death, the end, of what began in beautiful, hopeful promise brings anguish to the heart.

Oftentimes, those involved believe a formal divorce will be a cut-and-dried "the end," and both parties will go their separate ways, living happily ever after. Sometimes that is the case. However, especially if children are involved, the moments of anguish recur and play out as the parents find themselves grappling with difficult issues such as custody. Children are absolutely affected by divorce and often suffer. The parents—the two—have literally become one in their offspring, and, in truth, there is no easily separating that blending of genes and personalities.

Children suffer, may they be young or grown. When I was teaching high school, every year without exception teenagers with divorcing parents were nabbing tissues and crying on my shoulder. Rivers of ink went into papers expressing their bitterness at fathers who rejected and abandoned them. Or telling of how mothers were struggling as single moms, working to provide for and nurture them. The loneliness, heartache, and despair seemed overwhelming. Fix it, Lord. Fix it!

We can't fix it. "I'm leaving you. I just don't love you anymore." "I'm sorry, but I've fallen in love with someone else." "You are too into God and church." "Look, I just want to do some drugs and hang out with my buddies. You're a drag." And on it goes.

Oh, often, we try to fix it and even stay in the marriage, especially if we took our vows seriously and don't, ourselves, believe in divorce. However, even in those cases, the relationship is seriously fractured or broken. The "marriage" becomes two people living as roommates splitting expenses.

God created the idea of marriage with the intention that a man and woman would find their helper and the two would become one. "So they are no longer two, but one flesh. Therefore, what God has joined together, let no one separate" (Matthew 19:6). Yet early on, Satan managed to corrupt and thwart God's plans, and Jesus stated that as far back as Moses, provision had to be made for divorce, noting that "It was because your hearts were hard that Moses wrote you this law" (Mark 10:5).

Thankfully, the Lord is full of compassion and realizes we are but dust. He understands the motives, nuances, and necessities that lead to divorce. He sees and has compassion on the anguished hearts caught in such difficult situations. He loves us; he cares. He knows how Satan deceives us and leads us astray into circumstances we never expected and can't fully understand. "For the Lord comforts his people and will have compassion on his afflicted ones" (Isaiah 49:13). God be with us in these difficult situations.

Reflection

- Has your life, or someone's you love, been touched by divorce? Reflect on the ramifications of that event.
- From brokenness—be it a divorce or a loveless ongoing marriage—have you seen the Lord's comfort and compassion? In what ways?

Prayer thought: "Dear Lord, the creator of marriage, be mindful of our weakness and our hurt as so many of us struggle with relationships. Give us the ability to make wise choices and the strength to cling to you. Amen."

A Long Way Back

*And we know that in all things God works for
the good for those who love him …*

—Romans 8:28

My heart is grieving for a friend who was thrown from her horse and broke her lower back. Not only do I mourn for her, but for her husband and family. And for her many friends. Her husband has a major farming / cattle business to run. How he will manage while she is in rehabilitation and undergoes a long home recovery preys on his mind. The irony is that they barely get along after years of marriage. Previously, she even stated her worst nightmare was to be injured and have to depend on him. Her nightmare—at least for a while—has come true. She loves the Lord with all her heart; her husband has no use for "church things." She lies broken of body; he sits dejected, struggling in his mind. And most assuredly both ask the unknowable, "Why?"

Such tragedies affect not only those directly involved but also those who know and care about them. Most of us also struggle with the "why," even as we know God rarely grants us that knowledge. And so we gradually leave the "why" in order to watch, prayerfully, for the good that may come.

All things are obviously not good, but God brings good from all things in order to bless his people. As he will from this horrible life situation, though his ways are not our ways. We want to know *now* that she will recover completely and be her old self. That through this experience her husband will draw close to the Lord and know him. That is our vision of "good." However, perhaps she will always remain handicapped. And perhaps he will become bitter and angry, blaming God. The Lord, however, knows the outcome. We can rest assured.

Nothing can be rushed. All will unfold in God's perfect timing according to his will. We pray for patience and for faith, for "we know all things work together for good for those who love God …"

Reflection

- Recall, if you can, a bad situation which ultimately turned out much better than you expected. What did you anticipate? What ultimately transpired?
- Looking back, try to trace the ways, the steps God took to bring about the good result.

Prayer thought: "We praise you, Lord, for the way you help us get through all things, turning the bad into good. Thank you for all of your blessings in life. Amen."

Answered Prayers

*This is the confidence we have in approaching God; that
if we ask anything according to his will, he hears us.*

—1 John 5:14

Answered prayers are scary, and they usually entail responsibility. Pray for a house? Upkeep and cleaning. Pray for a job? Loss of freedom and shouldering of work. Pray for a car? Repairs, insurance, and gas. Pray for a dog, cat, horse? Constant care and feeding. Pray for a child? Oh, my ... you get the idea.

And whatever you do, don't pray for patience. God frequently seems to answer those prayers by placing people who so ask in situations that require endless patience. I assume his rationale is we learn to be patient by—what else?—exercising the need for patience!

Often, God answers our prayers with a "wait" or a "no," for he does understand the responsibility that can come with his saying yes. Are we ready to handle that? He sees the bigger, the complete, picture, and he knows what is best. And, of course, God works his will with a kingdom view. What, ultimately, demonstrates his great glory? The Bible makes it clear that challenges help us to grow and to depend upon him. Paul prayed three times, prayed fervently, for the removal of an undefined "thorn in the flesh." God's take on the situation? "My grace is sufficient for you, for my power is made perfect in weakness" (2 Corinthians 12:9).

Still, for us, it can be difficult, almost impossible, to understand. Those trapped in war zones cry out to God as bombs explode, starvation looms, and no help appears. Patients stricken by horrible ailments suffer helplessly, pleading for God's intervention. Children, while being abused and harmed, weep alone with feelings of abandonment. Why doesn't God step in and stop these things! Even the saints under the altar cry out "How long, sovereign Lord ... until you judge the inhabitants of the earth and avenge our blood" (Revelation 6:10)?

We can't answer any of these questions; some things must be understood through faith. And, of course, this is a fallen sin-laden world where horrible things happen to the wicked and godly alike. However, for the godly, there is the promise, the assurance, "And surely I am with you always, even to the very end of the age" (Matthew 28:20). He walks with us through the valley, the flood, the fire, the illness, the discouragement. Not necessarily around the challenges, but through them. Let us ever be bold in prayer, accepting God's answers and timing, accepting the responsibility God gives us, and being ever aware of his presence in our lives.

Reflection

- Honestly acknowledge those times when you, like the saints under the altar in heaven, have cried out, "How long, sovereign Lord?" What about those times so grieved your heart?
- Take time to find and ponder specific Bible passages that address such issues and let them speak to your heart. Meditate on God's hope and comfort.

Prayer thought: "Lord, sovereign Lord, how long will the evil in this world flourish? Father, help me to understand your ways—that they are not our ways. Give my heart comfort and assurance, even as I lament what I see all around me. Amen."

Section 4

And You Were Not Willing

Blessed are the peacemakers, for they will be called children of God.
—Matthew 5:9

Reconciliation
Let It Go
Flee Evil
Are You for Real?
Egoism and Pride
Sacrificial Love
Beware—Truth Ahead!
I Choose Not to See
Make It Better

Reconciliation

O Jerusalem, Jerusalem ... how often I have longed to
gather your children together, as a hen gathers her chicks
under her wings, and you were not willing.

—Matthew 23:37

I want to reconcile with a dearly beloved relative—and she will have none of it. The original rift caught me by surprise, was totally unintended, a misunderstanding I still do not really understand. Apology, offers to get together and talk, several years of reaching out at birthdays and holidays and of seeking a renewed relationship—all answered by silence.

The years are passing, no one is getting any younger, and family is precious. However, the aspect of the situation that brings tears to my eyes is all the missed opportunities for fun, laughter, and sharing.

How does this cutting one's self off from family and friends benefit her or anyone else? The entire point of it all eludes me, as previous joyful times are seemingly easily cast aside. One thing this situation does, however, is make me appreciate, in a small way, how Jesus must have felt as he gazed at the holy city of Jerusalem filled with his beloved people. He had guided the Israelites, protected them, instructed them, pleaded with them for centuries. "Hey, dear ones, I'd love to hear from you. Let us reason together. Let us have sweet fellowship. Let us share in gracious, blessed times of joy and prosperity."

And Jerusalem, the Chosen People, would have none of it. Jesus longed to open his wings as a hen does to her chicks, thereby providing warmth, closeness, and protection. "No!" was the answer, repeatedly. Or, perhaps worse, his people answered by ignoring the

71

Lord, their God. As Jesus gazed over the city, he knew the Romans were coming to wipe it off the face of the earth for a long time and to scatter the Jewish people for hundreds of years.

As I ponder estrangement in my own extended family, I know before too many years death will begin to claim us one by one, and the possibility of fellowship on this earth will be gone. Oh, loved one, how I've longed to work things out, to sit and talk, to enjoy harmony once again … and you will not.

Jesus knew, and I know, forced fellowship is no fellowship, and so there is nothing to be done but to weep, hope for the best, and move on. Let all of us, everywhere, prayerfully consider our relationships with others; and where needed, let us reach out to mend fences, heal misunderstandings, and forgive true wrongs. For healing comes only through forgiveness, and those of us in Christ are all of one body. We will be together in heavenly life. We might as well speak to one another here and now and praise his name!

Reflection

- If possible, with whom would you like to be reconciled? Why?
- What specific steps can you take to try and bring this about? If they won't respond, how will you come to terms with that?

Prayer thought: "Father, you know I long to reconnect with those I love but am estranged from. Give me the guidance and wisdom to deal with this heartbreaking issue. Amen."

Let It Go

◆◇◆

Since they have rejected the word of the Lord,
what kind of wisdom do they have?

—Jeremiah 8:9

Nothing pains and distresses the believer's heart more than seeing a loved one deliberately turn away from Jesus and his way, especially when at one point they seemingly believed. Now they not only reject but also ridicule.

"The Bible is inaccurate, mostly myth, and the entire Jesus storyline is highly improbable. While I'm not an atheist, I'm an agnostic now. I mean, there may be something out there, but we have no way of knowing," is how one of my loved ones stated his position.

The hearts of mothers, fathers, brothers, sisters, aunts, uncles, and others who love the rejecting person shatter. Frantic, unable to comprehend, we may fruitlessly resort to logical argument, scripture sharing, and dire warnings (you are going to hell!) in order to win the loved one to Jesus. Certainly, we pray—oh, how we pray.

And we question. Were they ever truly a child of God in the first place? If so, can they "lose their salvation"? Why would anyone taste of the joyful life in Christ and deliberately turn away? Sorry, but no easy answers are available. Serious study and soul-searching are required. One thing is certain—the grief Christians feel in such a situation is real and often beyond enduring.

It all comes down to faith. What choice have we but to turn the situation over to the Lord? It's impossible to argue someone, threaten someone, browbeat someone, manipulate someone into a saving walk with the Lord. Let it go. Sometimes, we really have no other option, especially if any mention of Jesus and Christianity sends our loved one into a tirade of reviling those things we hold most precious.

"Do not give dogs what is sacred; do not throw your pearls to pigs. If you do, they may trample them under their feet, and turn and tear you to pieces" (Matthew 7:6). Wisely let it go; give that unbelieving loved one to the Lord. Pray for them but also accept that there may be nothing you can do. Stop throwing the precious things of Jesus before that person to ridicule and trample in the mud. Stop opening your heart to continued savaging. Let it go; let God work. For he does understand the causes, reasons, and pain of the rejecting one's decision. He does know and is in control of the outcome. He is merciful and judges aright. There is no remedy within your power. Let it go. Have faith. Peace.

Reflection

- Consider—is there a loved one in your life who adamantly rejects Jesus? What have you done to try and reach them?
- How does the idea of "letting go" affect you? Does it make sense in your situation? Why or why not?

Prayer thought: "Lord, give us the ability to let go of trying to control, manipulate, or compel others, realizing that only you and your spirit working in them can bring about change. Let us entrust them to you. Amen."

Flee Evil

—◆◇◆—

*I keep my eyes always on the Lord. With him at
my right hand, I will not be shaken.*

—Psalm 16:8

She posted a short video on social media and encouraged me to watch it so I could "better understand her position." Given that I have been working with her on matters of faith for a while, and given my deep concern for her drift into atheism, I did so.

A chill griped my heart as I watched a group in Satanic robes placing a lighted candle on a pentagram. Ironically, the group's message was, "We are *not* Satan worshippers. We want to increase tolerance, do away with judgmentalism, and work toward inclusion of all people."

Deeply concerned, I expressed my dismay at her even considering opening herself to this dark, dark pathway.

"Did you watch it with an open mind?" she replied, obviously annoyed at my response.

After careful reflection, I responded, "No, not this time. Opening our minds to any influence of Satan, in any way, is something dangerous to do. I can't and will not do so. But I will be in prayers for you every morning, that you may be kept in God's hands."

In my Christian walk, especially in my work with this particular loved one, keeping the balance between open lines of communication and pleasing the Lord has been a challenge. As Christians, we are commissioned to go to, and work with, the lost, the searching, the hurting. Of course, it would be easier to shun those "not like us" and sequester ourselves with our fellowship of believers, but that's not God's plan. We are to be *in* the world, but not *of* the world.

As I have mentioned to my unbelieving friends, many strong advocates for Christianity started out as convinced atheists. (C. S. Lewis comes to mind.) However, it seems like a big difference between a questioning nonbeliever and someone deliberately opening their mind to satanism, in any form.

Kindly, politely, firmly there comes a time to assert, "As for me and my household, we will serve the Lord" (Joshua 24:15). Some things are not open to exploration; some things we are to flee, even at the risk of being considered close-minded. The good news is that the Lord is always before us and at our side. He will protect us from the evil one and guard our hearts. He will go with us into the battle for hearts and minds, knowing it may lead us into dangerous territory.

Interestingly, when I checked back just fifteen minutes or so later to see if there was a reply from my friend to my statement, the post was gone, deleted. Nothing more has been said on the issue, and we have since had several pleasant exchanges. I like to think my firm stance caused her to rethink the issue. I hope so. Regardless, God holds her, me, all of us, in his hand. That being the case, let us flee evil and turn to him.

Reflection

- Consider what areas in life you simply will not delve into due to Christian convictions. Why not?
- How might you respond to someone you know who encourages you to be "more open-minded" to ungodly things?

Prayer thought: "Oh, Father, lead me not into temptation, but deliver me, and the person I am concerned about, from evil. Amen."

Are You for Real?

◆◇◆

One who has unreliable friends soon comes to ruin, but there is a friend who sticks closer than a brother.

—Proverbs 18:24

How can you know someone for years and not know them? People can be so closed up, so unsharing, that they remain enigmas. They put others in the position of always guessing. What is he or she thinking? Feeling? What are his or her true beliefs? What does he or she desire from life? What are his or her goals and dreams? Hello—are you for real?

Even though you may see the person often, even deal with him or her daily, you remain ever and always essentially outside. There is no sharing soul to soul, mind to mind. The realization of the situation is hard and sad. Such people can be friends, family, spouses. At best, they are frustrating. At worse, they betray and deliberately seek to cause harm.

Which leads us to Peter and Judas, two biblical examples of people who were not really what they initially seemed to be. Interestingly, both men were close friends of Jesus; in fact, they were among the chosen twelve. Of course, Jesus knew them, knew their hearts. But what of the other ten close followers who sat at the Master's feet?

Oh yes. Peter. Great guy, best guy you'll ever meet. Hardworking, super fisherman. Strong. A tad impetuous, maybe at times hotheaded. Still, if a problem comes up, Peter will always have your back. Loyal is the word, there with you through thick and thin. An open sort of man. You always pretty much know what he is thinking.

Judas Iscariot? Honest comes to mind. I mean look, he was selected to be more or less the bookkeeper—treasurer for the group. Now I ask you, would someone unreliable be given the money bag?

Obviously, a smart person overall. And while practical—look how he protested when that lady brought extremely expensive perfume to anoint Jesus at that dinner—he had a generous heart. Remember how he pointed out the money could have been used to help the poor?

Really knowing someone. Difficult, isn't it? Peter didn't appear to be a guarded person at all, and yet there it was. That inner person capable of actually, repeatedly, denying his dearest friend, Jesus. Pointed out as one of Jesus's followers, he said, "No! No!" Even threw in a few curses and oaths for impact. To his great credit, he came to his senses, repented in bitter tears, and, having learned something extremely painful about himself, went on to better things.

Judas, now ... turns out he had been a thief all along, stealing from the treasury bag. Hidden, truly guarded, an enigma to the others. He shocked everyone, except Jesus, by revealing his true self via a treacherous act of betrayal. When remorse hit him, humility and seeking forgiveness evidently weren't in his makeup. Rather, he went and hanged himself. Betrayal led to self-murder.

We share life with people, thinking we know them. Thinking they are open and upfront like Peter. Thinking they are quiet, thoughtful, honest like Judas. And we don't know them. They may not truly let us in. They may surprise us or ever remain a frustrating mystery.

However, Jesus knows. Jesus understands our bewilderment in dealing with others, knows the great loneliness or hurt heart that may result. "Come to me, all you who are weary and burdened, and I will give you rest" (Matthew 11:28).

Reflection

- Who has fooled you in life by turning out to be quite different from who you thought they were? What did they do that wounded or bewildered you?
- How have you handled the situation? Do you hold a grudge, or are you working on forgiving?

Prayer thought: "Father, be with us as we seek to live with and understand others. Help us to be wise and to forgive. Amen."

Egoism and Pride

The person without the Spirit does not accept the things that come from the Spirit of God ...

—1 Corinthians 2:14

He doesn't listen; he doesn't learn. He hears, but he doesn't understand. He takes great pride in the results of a personality test. "I'm a dominant person. I'm a loner who doesn't work well with others. I'm brusque! And that's just the way I am ..."

Pride in these traits? Point out that he hurts people, he is rude, he is harsh, and he shrugs. "Well, my personality test says that's just the way I am. Fine by me. Don't need to change it, probably can't."

He never apologizes; he rarely compliments. He gets compliance by intimidation—be it ever so subtle—and manipulates by guilt. Perfectly willing to have others work and benefit him, he does as little as possible. He says he is a man of God. His various good works and charitable ventures in the past were undertaken in God's name—and undeniably aided others. However, he is rarely into God's Word, neglects Christian fellowship, and does not talk of God or a Christian walk.

In short, he presents a confusing picture. There are many like him. What are people to make of such a person? It is not our place to judge anyone's state of salvation or standing with God, so we don't and won't. We are, though, counseled to look for and assess the fruit. Given that the fruits of the Spirit are love, joy, peace, patience, kindness, goodness, faithfulness, gentleness, and self-control, we are to look for those attributes.

First Corinthians says the person who truly loves God is open to God's knowledge. To seek knowledge is to grow in the Lord. Where is knowledge to be found? Without doubt, the most important avenue of godly knowledge is to study—not just hurriedly read—God's Word, the Bible. As we learn of Christ's great sacrifice for us, our egoism begins to shrink, and our sense of humility begins to grow. There was and is nothing humans can do to earn salvation other than by believing, accepting, and trusting in Jesus. Understanding this, we then must do the hard part—admit we are pretty sorry creatures immersed in sin.

And this step, basically square one, stops the prideful cold. "What! Me admit I'm someone who sins? Me admit I'm not in charge, not good enough? Me admit I need God? No, there is nothing I need to repent of or ask forgiveness for." The process of rebirth, of becoming a child of God, is thwarted.

Besides being in the Word, we gain knowledge by fellowship with others of like precious faith. Successful cooperation with other flawed but seeking fellow Christians requires struggling with pride. Those who "know it all," who are "holier than thou," and who are not open to listening to others can cause endless trouble and hard feelings. That willingness to learn, to be kind, patient, gentle are all essential to successful Christian discipleship. And, no, it doesn't always come easily; but we who truly love God with openness, and who allow Spirit's work in our lives, can succeed and grow.

Reflection

- What ungodly traits do you struggle with in your life? Be honest. No one else needs to know!
- What spiritual fruit can you seek, with God's help, to replace these negative traits?

Prayer thought: "Lord, I can so easily see the faults of others. Help me, Lord, to see my faults. Give me the guidance of your Spirit, that I can grow in you. Amen."

Sacrificial Love

Follow God's example, therefore, as dearly loved children and walk in the way of love, just as Christ loved us and gave himself up for us as a fragrant offering and sacrifice to God.

—Ephesians 5:1–2

"I'm willing to love, as long as I'm not inconvenienced." Most of us have met these people; perhaps truth to tell, at times we are these people. However, for those who seek to imitate God and dearly love, outbreaks of disregard and selfishness are counterbalanced by awareness and regret.

And then there are the "others." It seems, sadly, that often people practicing sacrificial love are found and latched on to by their opposites—the "love if convenient" folks. The reasons for this would, and do, fuel many psychological studies and are beyond the scope of this meditation. The results, alas, are evident on a daily basis.

To truly love others, we must have empathy—the ability to feel what another living creature feels. The owner must be able to look at her hungry dog and see the pet's discomfort and longing. The "convenience only" person reasons, "I'm tired and want to sleep late. The dog can wait."

The loving parent responds to a crying child with attention, trying to understand and, if possible, alleviate the distress. The "convenience only" parent snaps, "Can't you see I'm busy? Stop crying, or I'll give you something to cry about."

The wife, who strives to love, though tired herself, has compassion on a sick husband and fills the hot water bottle, tucks in the blankets, and prepares the chicken soup. The convenience only person says, "Sorry you're sick. There's a can of soup in the pantry. Got a lunch date. Bye!"

The husband, who cherishes, takes off an afternoon from work to drive his wife to chemotherapy, sits with her, and takes her home. The "convenience only" husband prepares for work, heads out the door, and pauses a moment … "Hope your chemo goes well. Drive carefully."

Much pain is inflicted by those who love "as long as it's not inconvenient." Further, attempting to help them see what they are doing usually proves pointless. "Okay, talk, but I've gotta run in ten minutes" often defines their attitude.

So the victims are left to seek the Lord for answers, for ways to cope. And the Lord has words of wisdom. Patience, peace, reliance on God—not humans. Also, he gives the ability to see reality, not "if only" dreams. To give up on false hopes that "someday, if I try hard enough, he will cherish me, be kind, really care." Only God can soften the heart of another; we can't do it by being "good enough." Seeing this truth can lead to freedom for the one enduring the pain. For God never loves only if it is convenient. His love endures forever.

Reflection

- Think about a time when you experienced someone who loves "only when convenient." What seemed to motivate them? Have you found yourself being this way? Why?
- Ponder God's love. What does it mean that his love endures forever? Select a specific example of when you experienced God's enduring love.

Prayer thought: "Lord, forgive me when I have shown love only if it's convenient. Thank you for your enduring, never-ending love. Amen."

Beware—Truth Ahead!

*Above all you must understand that in the last days scoffers
will come, scoffing and following their own evil desires.*

—2 Peter 3:3

"Don't tell me what is true. Tell me what I want to hear."
Sadly, this seems to be the mind-set of many in today's
world. How totally discouraging this can be to those who seek truth.
Of course, seeking truth can be very uncomfortable, for truth can
illuminate the flaws and hypocrisies in our own souls. It takes true
humility, oftentimes, to hear and accept the truth. And for most of
us, humility is not a strong point. Humans, by nature, are full of
pride.

Truth may indicate to us that we are selfish. "Are you only volunteering in order to pad your resume?"

"Who, me? How dare you even suggest such a thing!" Well,
truth is …

Pride, however, will have us protesting and defending ourselves
vigorously. Truth may clearly point out a sin, which we previously
neatly wrapped up in pretty ribbons of self-delusion.

"I know appropriating a bit of the fund-raising money could be
considered stealing, but believe me, anyone who knows me will agree
I have put in many unpaid hours, driven many unreimbursed miles,
so it's only fair I get some compensation. If I told them, anyone
would agree, but there is absolutely no reason to bother anyone over
this trivial issue!" Right.

We avoid truth constantly, truth be told. Now wait—telling
that truth was just harsh! How unkind to say anything like that, even

if it is the truth! In these last days, scoffers, indeed, have come. In droves.

"'I am the way and the truth and the light. No one comes to the father except through me,' said Jesus" (John 14:6).

"How incredibly intolerant," chant the scoffers. "How bigoted. How exclusive. What is wrong with you Christians?" The truth is, there exists an absolute standard for right and wrong. The truth is, sin remains sin, even if society says otherwise. The truth is God loves everyone, but he also reigns as a God of justice. The truth is we cannot earn our salvation, not ever.

Therefore, if we claim, "I'm just as good as the next person, better than most," it doesn't mean a thing. Scripture says all have sinned; our works are as filthy rags before God. That is truth. We are—take note—to speak the truth in love. No ranting, raving, and judging that so and so is going to heaven or hell. No telling the truth with disdainful, gloating tones as we look down our self-righteous noses.

Undoubtedly, truth is a powerful and tricky thing. It makes us uncomfortable at hearing the truth if it results in holding a mirror up for us to face ourselves honestly. And speaking the truth is a challenge when in the midst of scoffers who ridicule us, label us as "haters" and turn away. Yet truth must be told, for it is truth that ultimately sets us free.

Reflection

- Pilate asked, "What is truth?" How would you have replied to him?
- Reflect on a time when you spoke the truth in a difficult situation. What happened? How did things turn out?

Prayer thought: "Father, have mercy on those blinded by Satan's lies, that they may be drawn by you into a knowledge of the truth. Amen."

I Choose Not to See

---

*For every animal of the forest is mine, and the
cattle on a thousand hills. I know every bird in the
mountains, and the insects in the field are mine.*

—Psalm 50:10–11

I don't want to write about this; it still hurts to recall the incident.
The actual events may seem trivial, but the surrounding implications are enormous. My parents let my beloved cocker spaniel die a slow, painful death. For years, I shouldered all the blame, until a wise counselor pointed out that I, as a young teen-ager, held very little power in the household.

My dog, pregnant, couldn't birth her puppies. She strained, cried, and whimpered for several days; and then the putrid, smelly discharge began as the puppies died. I had her up in my bedroom, trying to comfort her. Did I not understand what was going on? Did I understand and just block it out in a life filled with school and chores? Honestly, to this day, I don't know.

However, my parents had to know. My mother had birthed five children; she had to understand. My father ruled the house. Given our shaky financial situation, he most likely felt there was no money to spend on a dog. And so my dear pet died. We killed her slowly. Why didn't we just shoot her early on so she didn't suffer? It all hurts so. I have long asked the Lord to forgive us.

The bigger issue, though, is parents—people—who, from ignorance or hardening of their hearts, allow such things to happen. I'm not alone in this confusion regarding the behavior of people I think of highly. How do our hearts reconcile the dichotomy of "love" versus "cruelty"? How do we forgive and make sense of it all?

We understand by looking at the big picture and seeing where people "come from." What were they taught? How were they treated? What resources, strengths, and knowledge do they, or did they, have? And we remember that "as a father has compassion on his children, so the Lord has compassion on those who fear him; for he knows how we are formed, he remembers that we are dust" (Psalm 103:13–14).

This doesn't make poor choices or behaviors right or acceptable. By no means! However, it helps those who were wronged to understand, to let go, to forgive. Ultimately, God will sort it all out—and we will be freed from bitterness and anger.

Reflection

- If bearable, recall a great hurt from long ago. What was it? Who was involved? How did you view the incident then?
- From the advantage of time and greater understanding, consider what was truly going on. How can you—how do you—reconcile the event and forgive?

Prayer thought: "Lord, help us to understand that people, all of us, don't always clearly see our behavior and the ramifications it has. Forgive us, Lord, and help us to forgive others. Amen."

Make It Better

—◆◇◆—

*Then you will call and the Lord will answer; you shall
cry for help, and he will say, "Here am I."*

—Isaiah 58:9

Most of us have one (or many)—those loved ones who obviously are making wrong choices, who are broken and suffering. The niece with zero ambition. The nephew ever hustling to make the easy dollar. The spouse who spends hours in front of the television while life passes by. The child addicted to drugs, gambling, alcohol. Examples are many and varied.

Our options are limited; our frustration is great. How can we make them "see the light"? Let's face it, mostly we can't. No, we really can't. Ouch. Nagging hardens their attitude; they increasingly tune the nagger out, and resentment on both sides escalates. Attempts at control by such things as throwing out sugary food, alcohol, or drugs turn into a game of angry sneakiness. Shaming, name-calling, or hitting them with the Bible—literally or figuratively—often amplifies the behavior out of increased guilt, shame, and self-hatred. What can one do?

One way, the hard way, is an option that often succeeds. Turning the loved one over to God. Totally. Daily. Hourly. However often we need to. Praying for them, encouraging them, and asking God to work in the loved one's life. And then getting out of God's way, letting him work.

Now it's important to know God has great grace and forgiveness, but he also repeatedly stresses we may well reap the consequences of what we sow. As we stop rescuing the person from the big or small results of their behavior, we must realize our loved one may well face pain, hurt, poverty, illness—and we must not keep rushing in to "help." Prayerfully, fervently seeking God's wisdom, we must exhibit concern and kindness but not seek to control or manipulate. As simple as this may sound, standing on the sidelines in faith, letting God work, can be one of the greatest spiritual struggles in our life.

We can't fix it, but we know who can. God can work wonders in our loved one's life, for his Spirit can make changes in the person's very inner being, bringing him or her to an awareness of a need to change, to repent, and to walk with God. In truth, the desire must come from within the person; we cannot impose change from the outside. No external force can accomplish this truly life-changing transformation.

Passionate prayer, unconditional love, and a deep trust in the Lord can work miracles. Pray for it; then wait for it. Peace.

Reflection

- Consider someone you care about who is on a destructive path. What is their main problem? How are you feeling toward them? How have you tried to help?
- What results have you achieved by your method of intervention? What fears do you have about turning over the person to God, then stepping back?

Prayer thought: "Lord, I care so much for _____, and I am worried, Father. Help me to give my loved one to you. Please guide me day by day as you work in _____'s life. Amen."

Section 5

---◆◇◆---

My Grace Is Sufficient

My grace is sufficient for you, for my power is made perfect in weakness.
—2 Corinthians 12:9

Compassion
Deceit
Losing a Child
The Blessing of Difficulties
Sacrifice of Thanksgiving
Death Is Unnatural
Anxiety, Fear, and Worry
Caregiver

Compassion

My niece got punched the other day at work and ended up a bit bruised. "Now, Grandma, that's not nice," she scolded as she deftly avoided the ninety-year-old lady's flailing fists and got her into bed.

"All in a night's work." She shrugged when I asked her about the incident. "Sometimes I have to be pretty stern, because you can't allow people to act that way, but they can't really help it."

Five nights a week, she works in the nursing home's memory care unit, lovingly caring for Alzheimer and dementia patients. "How do you do it?" I have asked more than once.

"You know, I really enjoy them. I think God has just given me a heart of compassion. Actually, they often give me more than I give them."

Compassion. Caring. Giving a cup of cold water. Bearing one another's burdens. Jesus wept. He wept over Lazarus. He sat on the hillside and cried out, "Jerusalem, Jerusalem ..." Looking up into a tree, he told Zacchaeus to come down so Jesus could eat supper with him, an outcast tax collector.

"Woman, here is your son ..." Jesus was suffering on the cross, dying, and yet he made provision for his mother to be cared for by his friend, John. "Today you will be with me in paradise," he said to the thief hanging on the cross next to him. A thief probably getting what he deserved, but it didn't matter. He asked Jesus for compassion, and Jesus freely gave. And then at the end, he said, "Father, forgive them ... ," to those actually torturing him before he died.

And Peter, dear Peter, who had denied his Lord three times. There was Jesus on the shore, fixing the tired fishermen and apostles a delicious breakfast. They had been out all night working and undoubtedly appreciated a good meal! Peter. Did he hang back in shame, eyes averted? "Peter, do you love me?" Jesus asked. "Yes, Lord. Yes, Lord. Yes, Lord," the humbled friend replied (John 21:15–17).

Forgiven. Not only forgiven but given a commission to "feed my sheep." Peter was enveloped in compassion and entrusted with leading people into the kingdom, into the church which was coming into being.

Teachers, nurses, doctors, parents, workers in our churches. People in so many different roles in life showing great compassion. Exhibiting the ability to walk a mile in another's shoes, to put themselves into someone else's frame of reference. Thank God for compassion in this world. What would life be without it? Unfortunately, there are times and places where compassion is lacking, and what a horror that is. Just imagining a place absent of all compassion brings up images of what hell must be like, filled with the rawness of human nature and devoid of any influence of goodness.

"I love my patients," states my niece.

"I love my students," explains the harassed teacher.

"I love my children, my cranky neighbor, my enemy ... I can empathize with their struggles." Jesus said, "Do to others as you would have them do to you" (Luke 6:31). And so God's people give and receive compassion.

Reflection

- Do you know someone who exemplifies compassion for others? Consider what they do in the face of challenging situations to bless others.

- Reflect on a time or times when someone showed compassion toward you. What were the circumstances? How did their compassion assist you or make you feel?

Prayer thought: "Your compassion on me and others is beyond comprehension, Father. Thank you for loving me with patience and understanding. Amen."

Deceit

Dear children, do not let anyone lead you astray.

—1 John 3:7

S atan twists and corrupts, as much as possible, all things God created to be good and holy. Some of Satan's corruptions are obvious and, therefore, easy to avoid. Others, however, are subtle and difficult to detect. In Ephesians 4:11–15, Paul explains how Christ, through his Spirit, enables us to attain unity and knowledge, to be mature Christians instead of being easily deceived children, tossed about this way and that.

Clearly, Paul warns that teachers will come, even in the name of Jesus, with deceitful schemes. Further, in Ephesians 5:6, Paul commands, "Let no one deceive you with empty words." Empty words. Ah, now there is a deception to beware of (among many)! In our passion for Jesus, in our desire to convince others to follow him, we Christians are often easily led down the path of "empty words." We bring up God's love and goodness; they ask, "then why is there so much evil in the world?" And we are off. We mention the beauty and intricate wonder of God's creation; they counter with their adherence to random evolution. And away we go.

While being able to clearly articulate our beliefs is important, we also must not fall for Satan's deceptions. If he can deflect us from a central truth—that if a person does not have a personal relationship with Christ, nothing else matters—we can be deceived into fruitless arguments. In truth, what sins a person commits, what beliefs contrary to scripture they hold, or how they regard us doesn't matter. For without that saving relationship with Christ, they are not assured of salvation and a place in God's kingdom.

When, on the other hand, we recognize people are saved by *grace*, that it is God's gift, we will remain kind, loving and humble, and free of off-putting self-righteousness. And, oh my, it is self-righteous, condemning attitudes on the part of Christians that alienate many nonbelievers and drive them away. Avoiding the deception that we can argue people into faith in Jesus helps us approach others with love and respect. We can then focus on building relationships and exhibiting genuine loving concern. Of course, this is the last thing Satan wants to have happen.

How do we get to the point of recognizing and rejecting deception? I am totally convinced we, in and of ourselves, can't. However, as we study God's Word, pray and live in his Spirit, more truths will become evident to us. Jesus promises we will be given a spirit of discernment and will be enabled to see and understand. Of course, the ability to do that also may increase our sorrow as we realize the truly hopeless, sad state of the world. Therefore, it is imperative that we cling to our Savior, confidently believing that he has, indeed, overcome the world. "Then you will know the truth, and the truth will set you free" (John 8:32).

Reflection

- Think of a time when someone tried to argue you into agreeing with them. How did you feel and react? Did their tactics work? Why or why not?
- Honestly consider how you relate to and witness to others. Are your methods in line with Christ's and the Bible's teachings? How do you know?

Prayer thought: "Lord, I want to be affective in witnessing for you. Help me, in humility, to relate to people with kindness and respect. Amen."

Losing a Child

❖

For you created my inmost being; you knit me together
in my mother's womb. My frame was not hidden from
you when I was made in the secret place ...
—Psalm 139:13–15

How does one begin to write on this tragic topic? The grief sustained upon the loss of a child is unique to each parent, each person, involved in the loss. It matters not when the loss occurs. A miscarriage. An abortion, chosen and bitterly regretted. A toddler struck down by illness. A teenager killed in an automobile accident. A young adult slain in a foreign land while serving his or her country. An adult child taken, leaving elderly parents to grieve. Loss, sorrow, grief, and, always the unanswerable question, "Why, O Lord?"

We grieve not only the loss of the child but also all the potential embodied in that person. A great friend's only son was killed his senior year in a senseless automobile accident not of his making. Not only is he gone, but for his parents, there was the heartrending realization that their grandchildren, all future generations, would never come to be. "Why, O Lord?"

Another friend found out at age seventy-six that she has advanced cancer. She is alone, having had all three of her children and her husband precede her in death. The companionship of those children, the promise of someone dear to watch over her in her senior years, gone. "Why, O Lord?"

The death of an older adult, while sad, is somewhat tempered as we say, "Well, he had a good, full life." Not so with the death of a child or young person. They didn't really even get to experience life.

Tears flow, hearts grieve, and comforting words are hard to come by. Does God understand all this?

Yes, he does. If there is one area that God understands totally, it is the death of a son. And keep in mind, God knew ahead of time what Jesus would encounter and suffer. Jesus came anyway to this earth to redeem us. He experienced birth and brought joy to his mother's heart. However, early on Simeon, holding the baby in the temple, warned Mary, "A sword will pierce your own soul, too" (Luke 2:35).

Jesus grew and flourished into a fine young man when, at age thirty, he began his public ministry. How proud of him Mary surely was, and God himself declared, "This is my Son, whom I love; with him I am well pleased" (Matthew 3:17). Things seemed to be going well.

Before long, though, the time appointed for death arrived, and Jesus hung upon the cross. Seeing his mother standing near the beloved disciple John, Jesus said to her, "Woman, here is your son," and to the disciple, "Here is your mother." And from that time on, John took Mary into his home (John 19:26–27). God knows. He understands.

Grief. Such grief. We can't fix it, but we know who can. God promises to walk with us through the pain, the darkness, the ever-lingering sorrow and longing for the lost child. We need only throw ourselves on him, to be enveloped in his love and hope.

Reflection

- If bearable, reflect upon a child you or someone you know has lost. What emotions, memories, and longings result from such a death?
- How has the grief been handled? Has comfort been found? In what way? Is the grief still unresolved? What steps might you or they take toward giving it to the Lord?

Prayer thought: "Lord, our very souls agonize over the death of children, however old they may be. Parents, Lord, just assume they will outlive their offspring. To not do so is such a blow. Father, carry our grief for us when it is too much to bear, and, most importantly, give us your hope. Amen."

The Blessing of Difficulties

◆—◇—◆

A person can do nothing better ... than to find satisfaction in
their own toil. This too, I see, is from the hand of God.
—Ecclesiastes 2:24

God sometimes blesses us with moments of great joy—unexpected and unwarranted. In those times, gratefulness overwhelms our hearts and emotions, often resulting in tears of joy.

Isn't it interesting that usually—though not always—these joyful events arise amidst much effort, work, and often stress. Seems that it is out of difficulties God's gift of wonder springs forth. Not from ease, indolence, laziness, sloth, but from preparation, study, work, and effort.

If this be true—and it seems to be—why do we need fear or cringe from that which is difficult, given that is where the path often leads? Consider a few examples. The great joy of holding one's newborn baby culminates nine months of growth, concern, and hard labor. And any sports participant realizes the joy of winning, of being amongst the best, follows months, if not years, of steady and dedicated drudgery. Those serving in formal ministry well understand the hours put in, the sorrows encountered, the study and rehearsal to bring about moments of awe and wonder in the Sunday morning church service.

And lest we forget, "God opposes the proud, but shows favor to the humble" (James 4:6). Those moments of intense, unexpected, blessed joy happen to those of humble, grateful mien. The proud, who forget all good gifts come from God, think highly of themselves and expect, demand, that they triumph and win. Being exalted is their due! The humble, on the other hand, lean on the Lord, ask for guidance and strength, and focus on the process required, leaving the outcome to God. They work as unto the Lord, in his service, desiring a successful endeavor, but content regardless of the outcome. To them, unexpected triumph brings a sense of joy and gratefulness.

Therefore, let us work at those tasks God has set before us to accomplish, be they humble or grand. May God gift us with enjoying our work, as we focus on a job well done. If, then, triumphs, wins, and recognition come our way, they are but jewels in our crowns, gifts from the Lord on life's journey until we hear the ultimate triumph: "Well done, good and faithful servant ... come and share your master's happiness" (Matthew 25:23).

Reflection

- Think back on an accomplishment, win, or triumph you have experienced in life, be it great or small. What preparation and effort did it take to achieve that triumph?
- What goal have you currently set for yourself? What will be necessary to achieve it? What difficulties might you encounter?

Prayer thought: "Lord, as I plan and map out my course to achieve this goal, please quiet my mind and cause me to ask you to be with me and guide me. Amen."

Sacrifice of Thanksgiving?

◆◇◆

I will sacrifice a thank offering to you and call on the name of the Lord.
—Psalm 116:17

In the Old Testament, a thanks offering meant a specific, actual sacrifice. However, how in today's world might one give a sacrifice of thanksgiving? Merely saying "thank you" often doesn't seem enough. Nor does writing a check for 10 percent of all one's money. That seems too simple, too effortless. And why would it be any sort of a big deal to God?

I pondered this verse off and on for many a year when I would come across it in my Bible reading or devotional studies. And then today, the epiphany came. A glimpse of what it means. For over eight weeks, I have been caring for my little dog, Brella, after her eye surgery for glaucoma. The surgery went well, but the eye pressure kept spiking. After a two-week stay in the veterinary hospital, she was able to come home, but then a fungal infection set in. A regimen of various eye drops became the norm. Five a day, four times a day, for weeks and weeks …

At each veterinary checkup, reports were positive—things were getting better. And then the pressure shot up after a new eye drop was introduced, and it seemed we were back to square one. Seeing the devastation on my face, the doctor assured me it was most likely caused by the new medicine. He told me to stop using it and to return in two days to do a recheck. I cried as I drove home. My world seemed to be falling apart. "I'm tired of this, Lord. I want her to get healed. I know she's 'just a dog,' but she's a good dog, a dear companion, and she works serving you as a therapy dog to the sick and elderly. Why is this happening?"

On the way home, I had to stop at the church office to pick up a book, and I chatted with the secretary about a church member who is caring for her mom, who suffers with dementia. Prayers were requested. Other people were mentioned who were also facing life's problems.

As I said goodbye and got in the car, it became crystal clear to me. The sacrifice of thanksgiving is to *give thanks regardless* of one's circumstances. To realize that while one's problems, challenges and stresses are real, others also face similar problems. Some worse, some not so bad, but all frustrating and ongoing. Eventually, we all face death on this earth, suddenly or after a slow decline. We are to thank God in praise anyway, trusting that he knows what he is doing on a grand scale and holds us in his hand.

We give thanks in the face of life's slings and arrows, because we shall live eternally with Jesus in his kingdom, free of any evil, any sadness, any disease or injury. We give thanks even though it hurts, for there will be no more death someday, only the eternal joy of living with the Lord. We give God the sacrifice of thanksgiving, for all he has done for us.

Reflection

- What frustration, hurt, or challenge are you dealing with this day? What makes it so hard?
- In spite of the circumstances you are facing, try to pause and give an offering of thanksgiving to the Lord.

Prayer thought: "Lord, I praise you in spite of my struggles and trials. I am weary, Lord, to the bone with burdens, but I know you are with me. Have mercy on me and help me to remain ever faithful. Amen."

Death Is Unnatural

Precious in the sight of the Lord is the death of his faithful servants.
—Psalm 116:15

Death is unnatural; people instinctively feel this. Oh yes, we philosophically talk of the "cycle of life," and we work hard to come to terms with the inevitable here on earth. However, in our inner core, we think death is a frightful, imposing, unnatural thing. And—it is.

We were not meant to die. According to the Genesis account, death intruded via Satan, who sneaked into, if you will, God's perfect paradise. The puzzle is "why did God allow it"? Many have asked this question throughout the ages, wondering why death and sin were even permitted to come into being. We struggle to formulate an answer each time a treasured pet dies or we bury a beloved person. But, ultimately, who can truly know the mind of God? Certainly not us "we are but dust" humans.

The good news? Those who trust in Jesus need not sink into despair and hopelessness. Jesus and the New Testament writers repeatedly and persistently portrayed death as sleep. A time of waiting for the resurrection of our bodies to arise and live forever with the Lord. In fact, Psalm 116:15 says, "Precious in the sight of the Lord is the death of his faithful servants." Not that God delights in the experience of the bodily death of his followers, but rather that he so highly values them. He knows of their death; he knows the value of his people.

Just as his eye is on the sparrow and he sees it fall, so is his eye is on his people. Our loved ones, we, do not die alone and unnoticed. Rather, the Lord himself sees our physical passing, and he cares.

Sorrow, grief, heaviness of heart as we say goodbye to our loved ones, but we know we and they are held in the hands of Jesus. "Where, O death, is your victory? Where, O death, is your sting" (1 Corinthians 15:55)? We shall rise again!

Reflection

- Ponder the phenomena of death. How do you view it? What has been your experience with death?
- Write down a favorite verse or two that gives you great assurance and comfort when you ponder or are faced with death. What do you find especially comforting about this passage?

Prayer thought: "Oh, my Father, assure us that when you take us home through the door of death, you are there to greet us. Thank you that we will live forever where death will be no more. Amen."

Anxiety, Fear, and Worry

❖◆❖

The Lord is faithful and he will strengthen you
and protect you from the evil one.

—2 Thessalonians 3:3

Life sometimes seems like one endless series of anxieties and fears. Every stage has its unique set. Children fear being abandoned. Teens fear rejection and failure. Young adults fear not finding the right career or job, the right spouse, the right home of their own. Parents are anxious for their children's success and for their very lives. Retirees-to-be worry about having adequate resources to enjoy their leisure years. Older folks are anxious and fearful about selling the family home and moving into a care facility. And all ages are anxious and fearful about illness and death.

Where do these panic attacks, feelings of dread, and episodes of 3:00 a.m. worry come from? The evil one … the one who whispers in our ears, "God won't protect you and care for you. Oh, he *can*, but he won't. Just look around …" And we do look around; it appears Satan is correct. Consider, though, that part of our dismay comes because we believe some of the evil one's other lies. "God promised you no problems, no dread disease, no suffering here—and yet just look around." And we do. It's all there—the problems, disease, sufferings. The truth, though, is that Jesus clearly told us we will experience a variety of life's problem. We are not exempt.

Upon becoming being aware of our attacker's methods, our inclination is to fight back, to promise we will not lie in bed and worry, to not give in to anxiety. At which point, in trying not to think about our fears, we promptly think of them even more than before. We can't win.

No, we can't win, but Jesus can. I have repeatedly found that my efforts avail nothing. Therefore, when the evil one's dark suggestions enter my mind, I pray fervently for God to fill my mind with peace—and then I begin giving praise and thanks for all my blessings. I turn to God with prayer for protection, that anxiety will not overwhelm me. "I sought the Lord, and he answered me; he delivered me from all my fears" (Psalm 34:4).

With the Lord's gift of peace of mind, I, we, are enabled to face each day's challenges confidently and peacefully. Instead of being mentally paralyzed, we can think clearly and positively, continuing life's journey in peace.

Reflection

- When do your worry times seem to occur? What specific anxieties or worries keep recurring?
- Working with God in prayer, plan specific steps you will take when fear and worry try to capture your mind.

Prayer thought: "Lord, my Defender, hear my cry for help when anxieties, fears, and worry flood my mind. Send your peace that I may know quietness of spirit. Amen."

Caregiver

◆◇◆

We also glory in our sufferings, because we know
that suffering produces perseverance
perseverance, character, and character, hope.
—Romans 5:3–4

This morning, I feel like I totally lack the "caregiver gene." I've been nursing an injured dog for weeks, and I'm weary. Improvement is taking place but oh so slowly. She can barely see and can't go up or down the stairs, and I'm tired of carrying her twenty-something-pound body in and out.

I have decided not to carry her down the stairs to the fenced backyard at seven o'clock one morning to "do her business." Instead, I leashed her and took her out to the front yard. She just stood there and looked at me as if to say, "Nope, I need my freedom in the fence." So downstairs we went. I'm losing patience; I really am. That is so out of character, and I really love that little dog. Where is this irritation coming from?

As she nosed about the yard, I sank down into a lawn chair and watched the slowly brightening morning dawn. I let some tears slip down my face. She only wants, needs, her comforting routine. "Oh, Lord, she is so much like me! Whatever you do in my life, Lord, is just fine as long as it doesn't involve change. Do *not* disrupt my routine. If you do, I'll be like my dog—stubborn. I'll just stand there motionless and refuse to move."

The familiar routine is, well, familiar. Comfortable. Illness, job loss, family troubles, and new responsibilities all disrupt our life's patterns. Who—absolutely who—enjoys waiting endlessly in a hospital emergency room? The novelty of tending crying babies or sick toddlers wears thin at three o'clock in the morning. Cooking special meals, cleaning up messes, curtailing our activities to nurse the sick or elderly day after day, can make any one of us decide we lack the caregiving gene.

"Lord, I can't do this! I do not *want* to do this! Why me?" we wail in frustration and weariness. Serving others and doing our duty is not easy, not one bit. However, if not us—who? Of course, in many cases the time comes when we must step aside and rely on professional care. But in normal day-to-day living, it seems our turn to shoulder unpleasant responsibility eventually comes. And, often, we can't fix it, but we know who can. God gives us strength day by day. He tells us to give our burdens to him, and he will help us. What is it he said? To rejoice when we run into problems and trials? Why? Because, in truth, problems and trials help us to learn patience. And patience will serve us well as we seek to live a Godly life of service. "Peace I leave with you, my peace I give you" (John 14:27).

Reflection

- Think back to a time when life demanded you to assume the role of caregiver. It may have been the arrival of a new baby, injury to a family member, or responsibility for an older person. What were your initial feelings?
- At this point, what thoughts and feelings do you have about the experience? What have you learned, or what are you learning?

Prayer thought: "Lord, being responsible for the well-being of another can seem overwhelming. Even though our intentions are noble, resentments and fears do arise as life changes. Be with us, Lord. Give us perseverance, patience, and hope. Amen."

Section 6

Holy, Holy, Holy

And they were calling to one another: Holy, holy, holy is the Lord Almighty; the whole earth is full of his glory.

—Isaiah 6:3

Hole-y Like a Doughnut …
Rocks
All Things
From Death to Life
Opportunity
Sing Praise
In the Game
Jubilee

Hole-y Like a Doughnut ...

Wait for the Lord. Be strong and take heart and wait for the Lord.
—Psalm 27:14

Sitting here at the original Krispy Kreme doughnut works in Raleigh, North Carolina, I watch the assembly line of doughnuts slowly passing. My mind turns to thoughts of patient endurance. Ah, patience—something I, and others, struggle with.

How patiently the doughnuts progress past the viewing window. It all started in the back, where the workers kneaded large blobs of dough mix and, once it was properly stretched and pulled, turned it out onto tables for shaping.

Once properly shaped into little blobs, each doughnut-to-be was loaded onto the riser belt and began its journey. Up and down, they rode through the warming chamber, getting ever closer to the main conveyor as the heat caused the flat dough to gently rise and take on the shape of a puffy doughnut.

Ah, but the process wasn't over yet! The warmed doughnuts, white and pasty looking, were then tipped gently off the riser belt onto the main conveyor where they joined row after row of other doughnuts-to-be. And then, oh my goodness, now they are plopping into a vat of hot oil! Silently, they bob along, and far from being destroyed, the doughnuts emerge deliciously browned and beautifully formed.

Once more picked up by the main conveyor belt, the doughnuts journey onward until they slide through a silken veil of lovely white glaze, where they appear on the other side shining, sweet, perfectly crafted and ready to fulfill their purpose. Patient journey rewarded!

How like us as we progress in our Christian journey. There is no room for leaping ahead in the process of becoming a perfect Christian, a "little Christ." Hit the hot oil too soon, before we patiently endure the ups and downs of life with gentle heat applied, and we may be left flat, deformed. Life's blows, if we've not continually taken time to rise in faith, can destroy us.

And consider that even before we could begin rising as a doughnut, at the very beginning of our journey, there was all that stretching and shaping. How often we thought it would be nice to just stay part of the big lump of humanity, but then we would never have become a doughnut! Still, being formed into a "little Christ" often sounded like it would be unpleasant. All that pinching and squeezing!

And about that hot oil—that trial by fire, that ordeal of suffering in a hard place. Let's not patiently endure *that*! What? The trial is essential to go from raw to being a recognizable "little Christ"? Nope, I think it's best to stay a "raw" lump of humanity, even if that does eventually lead to being discarded as unusable. Wait, okay—I don't want that, so it's bravely into the hot oil. After all, the Master Baker stands on watch. All will be well.

Ah, out of the oil. Now a recognizable "little Christ," a Christian progressing on through life and then … up ahead … that final journey through a white veil of what? Can't quite see what's on the other side, but here goes … to emerge shining, sweet, complete as a perfected Christian ready to join the saints in heaven and fulfill our purpose. Each step of the journey, each part of the progress, patiently completed.

We were afraid to leave the big lump, but we put ourselves in the Master's hands to be shaped. We endured the heat of daily life, which raised us up into his resemblance. We endured life's trials and kept on going. And then, through death's veil into God's glory, holy!

Let us, like the doughnuts, progress patiently. God bless.

Reflection

- Recall the time when you decided to step out, believe, and risk being shaped into a "little Christ." What were your thoughts and feeling then ... and now?
- If you have not yet made the decision to be a Christ follower, what is holding you back? How might you address this issue?

Prayer thought: "Lord, I join you in the journey to become like you through faith, knowing there will be challenges ahead. Thank you, Lord, for being with me regardless of what comes, that I might live with you forever. Amen."

Rocks

*Have mercy on me, my God, have mercy on me, for
in you I take refuge. I will take refuge in the shadow
of your wings until the disaster has passed.*

—Psalm 57:1

On my desk are two rocks, given to me by Christian friends. The one on the left, taken from a stream, is unpolished and rough. A cross, done in red paint, graces it. On the right is an onyx stone, beautifully polished. In gold tone, the word *joy* is etched into it. They are a daily reminder that, in life, the roughness of the cross—the suffering—is a companion to the beauty of joy. After the ugly, the beautiful comes.

To the unbeliever, it often seems odd that those living in Jesus and filled with the Holy Spirit will say, "Yes, that was a horrible event in my life, but looking back if I had the chance to avoid it, I wouldn't. From that dark time of trial, I experienced the love and awareness of Jesus like never before."

As we ponder suffering, illness, death, separation in this world, let us be ever drawn back to the "rocks." After the cross comes the joy. The joy of acceptance and salvation. The joy of experiencing how the Holy Spirit did, indeed, pray for us when we absolutely could not pray. The joy of looking back and seeing how God worked to bring good out of all those horrible events. The joy of looking forward to eternity with Jesus.

Of course, sometimes the rough rock—the disastrous event—crushes a person. And, for them, no joy follows. Hearts harden, anger and fury block any conversation with God, the Holy Spirit is grieved, and life figuratively or literally is destroyed.

Which leads us back to the "why" question we know we can't answer. Why does one heart break under trial and another eventually find joy? We have no choice but to leave some things to God and his knowledge, and to quietly trust God's assurance. As 1 Corinthians 2:16 reminds us, "Who has known the mind of the Lord, so as to instruct him?" We know God is faithful through it all. Even as we lie seemingly crushed under life's rocks, we know that this, too, shall pass, and joy shall come. "The Lord will be your everlasting light, and your days of sorrow will end" (Isaiah 60:19).

Reflection

- Reflect on the hardest trial you have faced in your life. Did it lead to bitterness of spirit, or to growth in faith?
- Why do you feel you responded to this trial in the way you did? In what ways did you see God's hand working in your life?

Prayer thought: "Lord, in times of overwhelming trials, hold us close and keep us in your love, that we may know true joy. Amen."

All Things?

And we know that in all things God works for the good of those
who love him, who have been called according to his purpose.
—Romans 8:28

How does this work? I mean, I see and experience how a series
of seemingly unrelated events, many of them *not* good, work
together *for* good in my life and in the lives of others. I've stood back
in awe and thought, "Wow! How in the world did God work that all
out?" It's beyond comprehending.

Well, exactly. The human mind can't understand it. We humans
can get a glimpse of the true complexity, but only a glimpse. Consider
people who design and code complex computer programs, programs
that can fly planes, drive cars, do medical wonders. Humans can and
do touch on God's ability to interweave complex processes and create amazing results. However, to bring good from a series of bad?
Hmmm ...

As I pondered this issue, having just recently experienced how
a series of bad things brought forth good in my life, the sun was rising on a lovely day. I sat quietly in my yard with my dogs. A herd of
deer was grazing across the way, and a cardinal landed near my chair,
chirping. That's when I realized the "how" was truly beyond me, but
then I shouldn't be surprised. Think about it ... God was able to
design the entire universal system, making all aspects of it interweave
and function smoothly.

God has created endless amazingly complex systems all around
us, from the grandeur of space to the smallest of microbes. The complexity, the incredible interaction of it all, staggers the imagination.
He designed DNA codes in all living creatures that makes them—

us—what we are. Endless coordinated procedures keep us breathing, seeing, digesting, moving, thinking. We serve an awesome God.

"The heavens are yours and yours also, the earth; you founded the world and all that is in it" (Psalm 89:11). Surely and faithfully, this Creator of all things is more than able to take the threads of dire, bad, unpleasant incidents in our lives and the lives of others and weave them into ultimate good for his children.

"You will be secure, because there is hope; you will look about you and take your rest in safety. You will lie down, with no one to make you afraid, and many will court your favor" (Job 11:18–19). May we rest assured that all things certainly may not be good, but God will use all things to bring good to his dear children. Peace.

Reflection

- Ponder a "complexity of creation" you find particularly amazing. What is it? Why does it interest you?
- Remember a specific time in your—or another's—life when good came from a complex, seemingly bad situation or event.

Prayer thought: "Dear Lord, I stand in awe of your creation and how it all works in harmony. Thank you for working harmony in my life. Amen."

From Death to Life

❖

For the Mighty One has done great things for me—holy is his name.
—Luke 1:49

To better grasp what a mighty thing God has done for us through the death of his Son, let us carefully consider our plight if he had *not* given us a second birth into salvation.

We would be spiritually dead, with no God life in us. Creatures of the finite earth, we could enjoy and achieve only those things related to this world. Some people would reach great and lofty heights; others would achieve not so much. We would remain, however, simply part of the created creatures—nothing more. For there would be no God-life in us, no Holy Spirit. Further, being spiritually dead, we would be totally unaware that something more was possible. Unaware of something beyond, of something missing.

Not being aware of our spiritual deadness, we would not and could not make any effort to reach out to God or to become spiritual creatures. And, unfortunately, that is the state of many people in the world today. They remain dead to God.

Understanding this unawareness, this helplessness, is crucial to fully appreciating what Jesus, through his death, has done for us. We could do nothing to initiate a relationship with God, nothing to save ourselves. Something dead has no awareness, no life, and, therefore, no ability to change anything.

It was, and is, all God's work. God's decision and desire to take us beyond created physical life into a realm of spiritual life. To, in fact, adopt us into his family. Christ's death enables us to be born anew into this blessed state. His working and prompting within us enables us to hear his voice. Once aware, once we obtain a glimmer of eternal life with him as our shepherd, only then will we desire to seek him. Jesus said, "I am the good Shepherd; I know my sheep and my sheep know me" (John 10:14).

Once we are followers of Jesus, we become truly alive to God and his kingdom. He sees us as his family members, as beings beyond mere earthbound physical creatures. As a wise Christian friend explained it to me, "It's as if all of humanity is black and white. Then God touches someone, and that person suddenly bursts into radiant color." From death to life, we are set free!

The Mighty One has done great things, indeed. He has brought me to life and adopted me—a formerly dead thing—into his family. And it was all his doing, his plan, his design. Amid my "whys" at life's sorrows, pains, and frustrations, let this ever be the biggest why ... the why that asks, "God, why did you ever choose to come pay the blood atonement for me and my fellow humans? Why did you redeem us?" And that is a "why" that God has chosen to answer. "For God (I) so loved the world that he (I) gave his (my) one and only Son ..." (John 3:16).

Reflection

- Create a list of what the spiritually dead people esteem most in this life.
- Now create a list of things the redeemed child of God holds as most dear. Compare your two lists and ponder the differences.

Prayer thought: "Father, I am truly blessed to be a part of your family, to be a child of yours. Help me to ever be faithful to hear and heed your voice. Amen."

Opportunity

◆◇◆

Be still, and know that I am God.

—Psalm 46:10

And now I pause, for I am overwhelmed. Overwhelmed by God's goodness and his provision of opportunity. Overwhelmed at his answers to my prayers, I ask, "Lord, what direction am I to take? What do you want me to do?"

For so long, it seemed, there was silence. And then a revelation. Things fell into place. I'm overwhelmed with awe, gratitude, and thankfulness. The specific event—an interview to work with a local hospice. The opportunity came out of the blue, and I wasn't at all sure I was interested or able to take on this work. As the interview unfolded, it became evident they weren't answering my prayers, but rather I was answering theirs! It is, for me, frightening and humbling to realize God is using me to answer someone else's need. Rather scary. Very scary. Very awesome. A great responsibility. Too clearly specific; I think I prefer God in the abstract, at a distance!

As my interviewer went down her list, we both stopped and stared in silence. For each of her desired needs, I had the ability to meet them. Now training and details will be set in motion, and while I have apprehensions, I suspect God has the family needing me already in mind.

After the interview, I came to sit quietly on the overlook deck by my favorite local lake and watch the hawks soar high above the water before going home. I need to be still, to give praise, to absorb God's greatness—and also to work through what this new commitment will mean to my current schedule. I strongly suspect I'll need to eliminate some less important activities in order to make time for the most important activities. Sometimes, one must let go.

After writing these, my thoughts, I shall just sit still and be for a few minutes. Just *be* in the Lord, praising him for his mighty works. Hopefully, God will fill my quietness with his assurance and thoughts as we enjoy quiet fellowship. Let the adventure begin. Sing praise for opportunities!

Reflection

- What opportunities has God provided for you over the years?
- Select one and ponder how it came about, your reaction, and how it has turned out.

Prayer thought: "Dear God, here I am—use me. Lead me into the works You have prepared for me. Amen."

Sing Praise

❖

Praise the Lord. How good it is to sing praises to our God ...
—Psalm 147:1

Mom was restless and disoriented, secure in the Christian-oriented nursing home where she now lived in the Memory Care Unit but insecure in her mind. Dad had cared for her in their home as long as it was safe, but that time had ended. Dementia was winning.

During my visit that day, we walked the halls endlessly, she pushing her wheeled walker ahead of her, I strolling at her side, hand on her shoulder. When we went outside on the patio, she immediately wanted to go back inside. Once inside, she immediately wanted to go outside. And so it went.

"I want to go home," she repeatedly whispered in an anxious voice. Yet if I drove her to the house for a short visit, she paced about, whispering, "I want to go home." I couldn't help but wonder if heaven was calling her; she had walked with the Lord all of her life.

We walked; and the haunted, harried expression on her face only intensified. It broke my heart. The staff workers greeted her respectfully each time we passed the centrally located nurses' station, as we headed down yet another hallway. They liked Mom and always said she was a gentle, easy person to care for. Mostly, she ignored them and kept on walking.

She wasn't tiring, but I was, so I gently eased her toward the large activity sunroom where there were chairs to rest in. Once there, the view out the window held her attention briefly, and then she was pacing yet again. Clearly, she was not having one of her good days. I let her roam about the room as I headed over to the piano, eager to sit for a moment. Lost in thought, I absentmindedly began to softly play "Jesus Loves Me."

My heart stopped, even as my fingers continued the song. For behind me, clear and strong, my Mom's voice rang out. "Jesus loves me this I know, for the Bible tells me so …"

On she continued, singing every verse accurately, her voice never wavering. Tears were streaming down my face, but I kept playing. "I shall live with him on high. Yes, Jesus loves me …" Her voice went silent. In the doorway, several staff members were standing in amazement, attracted by the singing. "We have never heard Shirley sing before," one nurse said in an awed voice. "What a gift she has given us."

Mom didn't say another word as we went back to her room, and I helped into bed for her nap. She died not long after that wondrous visit. A marvelous gift, indeed—her gift of praise to God in song. God's gift to me, one I will never forget.

Where are our loved ones, really, when their brains are being slowly destroyed by disease? Since this event, I've learned that music, song, often triggers memories in these patients. What a mystery it all seems to be, even as research continues to try and help us understand.

One thing we do know. God understands it all perfectly. He holds the minds, the souls, the personalities of all those lost in such tragic circumstances. As we walk beside our loved ones, attend to their needs, and suffer in our very souls as they slip away, we can know "the Lord's got this." We can't fix it, but we know who can.

Reflection

- Has dementia or Alzheimer's affected your life or the lives of people you know? In what way?
- Have there been moments in your life similar to the one in this meditation, where God has given a sudden and unexpected blessing? Reflect on such times and give praise to the Lord.

Prayer thought: "Lord, Father, thank you for all the times you have sent the gift of unexpected blessing into our lives. Thank you, Lord, for songs amidst sorrow. We praise you. Amen."

In the Game

*Thanks be to God. He gives us the victory
through our Lord Jesus Christ.*

—1 Corinthians 15:57

Let's face it. I often drive my more competitive friends crazy. To them, winning is the entire point of being on the team or entering the contest. "It's the competition, Stupid!" Now I'll admit that getting the nod for first place—or any place—brings me satisfaction at having someone acknowledge my efforts. I work hard to do things well and right. However, I'm also perfectly satisfied just knowing I did a good job and remaining one of the humble ribbon-less losers! For me, it's not the winning; it's the privilege and blessing of being in the game.

In my horse-owning time of life, I'd always sweep into the show arena proud and thankful I could even be there, no matter the results (especially if I didn't fall off). Intensely aware of how fortunate I was to own a fine horse, to have its companionship, and to experience all the day-to-day challenges, the ride was more than enough reward. Likewise with my show dog. Just being at the show meeting interesting people, talking dogs, and bonding with my dog made the day. Ribbons, if they came along, were just nice extras.

Perhaps you are similar to me. You'll never play at the Master's, not with your golf game! Being drafted into the NBA isn't going to happen. You won't ever be the featured soloist for the Sunday morning choir ... and it doesn't matter. It's the joy of being a part of something you love and enjoy, the joy of being in the game, that counts.

Our walk with Christ on this earth is similar. We know, going in, that our ultimate victory, our reward, our triumph will not be in this life or in this world. We run a race day by day, rejoicing at being allowed to participate, while setting our hope on heavenly victory. Alongside others of like-minded faith, we enjoy our labors even amidst blood, sweat, and tears. We're partners on the same team as Jesus in this game of life, working to bring his kingdom to earth. We strive to help others join us in the endeavor that they might experience the peace and blessings we know.

And some glorious day, we'll complete our earthly participation, cross the finish line, and hear the Judge say, "Well done, good and faithful servant" (Matthew 25:21). At long last, victory! Lord, we humbly thank you for just allowing us to be a member of your team, to just get in the game. Keep us faithful until the end.

Reflection

- Are you highly competitive or not so much? Why do you think you are this way?
- Reflect on the race of life God has set for you to run. What, to your mind, indicates you are doing well in your race?"

Prayer thought: "Lord of the Race, give me strength and dedication to pass the finish line, having not grown weary, and to ultimately hear your voice of praise. Amen."

Jubilee

---◆◇◆---

Holy, holy, holy is the Lord God Almighty,
who was, and is, and is to come.

—Revelation 4:8

The two-mile ALS Association's Walk to Defeat ALS (amyotrophic lateral sclerosis) has just ended, and I sit recovering in the original Krispy Kreme doughnut shop here in Raleigh, North Carolina, with a cup of hot coffee and a blueberry cruller, resting my tired feet. I participated in honor of a dear friend and his wife, who deal with this horrid disease daily.

As I reflect on the morning, watching raw doughnuts ride down the assembly line into the cooking vats, other walkers wearing ALS logo shirts drift in and out, nodding and smiling at one another. "God is so good," I ponder. "So good. Look at all these folks, a small part of a larger group of people who care about goodness and compassion. Hundreds of people joyfully walking together proclaiming *hope* in the face of tragedy. Regardless of Satan's handiwork of disease and sorrow, these people are banding together and refusing to sink into despair. Here, then, is a foretaste of Jubilee, of rest after a long time of labor and challenges."

All over the world throughout the ages, God's people have stood bravely proclaiming hope. "It's coming," we assert. "Jubilee!"

"He is not here. He has risen," declared the angel (Matthew 28:6). Jubilee! Rejoicing! For in that moment of resurrection, God fixed forever what humans can't. He fixed it! We can't fix it, but he did. The work of redemption was finished. Death, misery, all of life's sorrowful challenges. We became free in Jesus. Whether we are destined to walk through physical death's doorway, or Jesus comes before that event to take us home, we are free. Jubilee!

"They will see his face, and his name will be on their foreheads" (Revelation 22:4). We shall see the face of Jesus. "Then my soul will rejoice in the Lord and delight in his salvation" (Psalm 35:9).

Even before these longed-for events, while we still navigate life's challenges here on earth, let us celebrate in Jubilee, for our eternal life has already begun. This very day Jesus gives us peace, love, and joy. We receive strength and guidance. And when we do go home at last, there will be no evil there, no tears, no death or mourning or pain … no darkness. Jubilee! Let us rejoice. "Come, Lord Jesus" (Revelations 22:20)!

Reflection

- How do you envision heaven? Jot down or ponder your imaginings. Perhaps find descriptive Bible passages that further your insights.
- What will be, to you, the grandest thing in heaven? Whom would you like to talk with? What might you wish to do?

Prayer thought: "Come, Lord Jesus. Bring your justice, mercy, and salvation to this fallen world. And for your joyous promises, and my salvation, I lift up my heart and voice to you in Jubilee. Amen."

About the Author

———————◆◇◆———————

Sandra Roberts Still's diagnosis, treatment, and survival of cancer radically changed her walk with Christ. From knowing *about* Jesus, she began to know him in a dynamic relationship. Retired from thirty plus years of teaching high school English, she currently serves as a commissioned Stephen Minister, hospice home volunteer, and therapy-dog handler visiting people in need of a comforting presence.

Faced with difficult challenges in her life and the lives of others, one constant kept emerging—the awareness that people can't fix it, but God can. Hope, peace, joy, and anticipation of eternity with the Lord consistently radiated through the most hopeless situations. In her book of meditations and reflections, Ms. Still shares some of her experiences in the hope that others may get a glimpse of God's glory.

A national board certified teacher, Sandra also holds a MEd degree in counseling and guidance and a bachelor's degree in education. She lives with her two Dandie Dinmont terrier therapy dogs and husband, Ronald, in Garner, North Carolina.

CPSIA information can be obtained
at www.ICGtesting.com
Printed in the USA
LVHW090251210821
695734LV00004B/456